BENNETT'S GUIDE to the BIBLE

BENNETT'S GUIDE to the BIBLE

Graphic Aids and Outlines

Boyce M. Bennett

THE SEABURY PRESS · NEW YORK

1982
The Seabury Press
815 Second Avenue
New York, N.Y. 10017

Printed in the United States of America

Scriptural quotations contained in the text are taken from the
Revised Standard Version of the Bible. Copyright (c) 1946,
1952 by the Division of Christian Education of the National
Council of Churches of Christ in the U.S.A.

Library of Congress Cataloging in Publication Data

Bennett, Boyce M.
   Bennett's Guide to the Bible.

   1. Bible--Outlines, syllabi, etc. I. Title.
II. Title: Guide to the Bible.
BS592.B46   220.6'1   82-3292
ISBN 0-8164-2397-0   AACR2

Illustrations by Ruth Soffer based on research by Boyce M. Bennett

Original art by the author on pages 10, 14 (map), 34 (skeleton),
36 (locust), 42, 89 (calligraphy), 92, 96(everyday life, kingship,
law), 99.

T A B L E   O F   C O N T E N T S

PREFACE

When geographers set out to study unexplored continents, they inevitably suffer the misfortunes of those who go into unknown territory. They make many wrong assumptions about the land in which they find themselves; they make many wrong turns; and, at times, they get completely and thoroughly lost. On the other hand, after they have completed their work, those who set out to explore the same continents for themselves will have the benefit of all the work that has gone on previously. They will know certain facts about the climate; they will know what geographical features to look for; and they will have some general road maps to keep them from getting lost.

If we approach the continent of the Bible as if we were the first to have encountered it, we will, no doubt, find it an exciting experience. But we will also be subject to some serious frustrations. We will find ourselves making many wrong assumptions about this strange new territory; we will make many wrong turns; and, at times, we will get completely and thoroughly lost. On the other hand, the frustrations can be cut to a minimum if we avail ourselves of some of the information obtained by those explorers who have gone before us.

It is the purpose of this volume to furnish the students of the Bible with an overview of the biblical continent itself and to provide a survey of the equipment that is needed when undertaking such an expedition. It is important to know in general what one will meet before one meets it (thus the section entitled VISUAL OUTLINES FOR THE BOOKS OF THE BIBLE). It is important to have some kind of road map to keep from getting lost in the forest of biblical history (thus the section entitled THE HISTORICAL TIMELINE OF THE BIBLICAL PERIOD). It is also imperative to have some kind of familiarity with the various instruments which will be used in this exploration (thus the section entitled THE TOOLS OF BIBLICAL CRITICISM).

The approach taken in this volume has been largely visual. Some people
tend to think visually more readily than others, but even those who tend
not to think in visual terms are able to benefit by the visual presentation
of those who do. The imagery employed in these pages is, in many instances,
a kind of visual "short-hand." Images are used to stand for whole complexes
of verbal ideas. The temptation in such a presentation is to over-simplify
the issues, and such over-simplification can be misleading. However, if
beginning students are able to grasp the basic principles in an over-simpli-
fied form, it is then possible to go on and explore the more complex realities which lie behind that over-simplification. The only alternative is to
plunge immediately into the more complex realities with no idea of the over-
all structure. Frequently, that is to invite disaster. So it must be clear
that the detailed study of the content of the Bible, the history of the
biblical period, and the tools of biblical criticism must be undertaken
in the appropriate introductions to those disciplines. This volume is
meant to accompany those introductions, and to act as a guide to the un-
familiar territory with which they deal.
NOTE: The illustrative material in Parts I and II reproduces, whenever
possible, the best archaeological knowledge about the actual clothing that
would have been worn at each time and place. The size of the figures in
Part II indicates their relative importance in the Biblical narrative.
Where little or nothing is known, the details have been deliberately left
vague.

In Part I the figures also serve a secondary purpose: by graphically
indicating the divisions of each book of the Bible, they can serve as aids
to memorization or to the understanding of the actual structure of the book.

I.
VISUAL OUTLINES FOR
THE
BOOKS OF THE BIBLE

VISUAL OUTLINES
OF THE
OLD TESTAMENT

1	Creation (P)		
2	Creation (J)	Adam and Eve	
3	Fall		
4	Cain and Abel		
5	Generations of Adam		Primeval Period
6	Ark built		
7	Rain falls	The Flood	
8	End of Flood		
9	Rainbow Covenant		
10	Generations of Noah		
11	Tower of Babel, Descendants of Shem		
12	From Ur to Egypt		
13	Abraham and Lot		
14	(Four Kings, Melchizedek)		
15	Covenant of Abraham	Abraham	
16	Hagar bears Ishmael		
17	Circumcision of Abraham		
18	Three visitors at Oaks of Mamre		
19	Destruction of Sodom and Gomorrah		
20	Abraham, Sarah, and Abimelek		Patriarchs
21	Birth of Isaac; Abimelek and Beersheba		
22	Abraham's faith is tested	Isaac	
23	Burial of Sarah		
24	Isaac marries Rebekah		
25	Death of Abraham; Birth of Esau and Jacob		
26	Isaac, Rebekah, and Abimelek		
27	Jacob cheats Esau and flees		
28	Jacob comes to Bethel		
29	Marries Leah and Rachel	Jacob (Israel)	
30	Jacob cheats Laban		
31	Jacob flees from Laban		
32	Jacob wrestles with an angel		
33	Jacob meets Esau, arrives at Shechem		
34	Seduction of Dinah		
35	Jacob goes to Bethel		
36	Descendants of Esau		

37	Joseph sold into slavery	
38	Judah and Tamar	
39	Joseph in Egyptian Prison	
40	Chief Butler forgets Joseph	
41	Joseph becomes overseer of Egypt	
42	Brothers come to Egypt	Joseph's Story
43	Brothers bring Benjamin to Egypt	
44	Benjamin retained	
45	Joseph reveals who he is	
46	Jacob comes to Egypt	
47	Jacob settles in Goshen	
48	Jacob's last words	
49	Blessing of Jacob; Jacob dies	
50	Jacob buried; Joseph dies	

Ch.	Content			
1	Israel in Egyptian bondage		Introduction	
2	Moses born; goes to Midian, marries		God prepares to save Israel	
3	Burning bush			
4	Return to Egypt			
5	Confronts Pharaoh			
6	Call of Moses (P); Genealogy of Aaron & Moses			
7	Nile polluted	Signs of the plagues		The deliverance
8	Frogs, gnats, flies			
9	Plague on cattle, boils, hail			
10	Locusts, darkness			
11	Death of first-born told			
12	Passover, Israel begins to leave Egypt	The Exodus		
13	Succoth to Etham			
14	Crossing of the sea			
15	Songs of Moses and Miriam			
16	Manna	On the way to Sinai		
17	Moses strikes rock for water			
18	Jethro visits; Moses appoints judges			
19	Moses talks to God on Sinai	The Covenant		Mount Sinai
20	Ten Commandments			
21	Laws for the Israelites	Book of the Covenant		
22	Property rights			
23	Festivals			
24	People agree to Covenant			
25	Ark, table, lampstand	P version of cultus		
26	Tent, wooden frames, veil, screen			
27	Brass altar, the courts, the lamp			
28	Ephod, breastplate, robe, diadem, turban, coat			
29	Consecration of the priests; the altar			
30	Altar of incense, poll tax, brass laver, oil, incense			
31	Appointment of craftsmen, the Sabbath			
32	Golden calf; tablets broken	Moses restores covenant		
33	People begin to leave Sinai; Moses and God talk			
34	Two new tablets (J's cultic decalogue); Moses transfigured			
35	Sabbath, the offering; the craftsmen	P cultus is effected		
36	Tabernacle: tent, wooden frames, veil, screen			
37	Ark, table, lampstand, altar of incense			
38	Brass altar, brass laver, court of tabernacle			
39	Priests' vestments			
40	Tabernacle is erected			

1	The burnt offering	
2	The cereal offering	
3	The peace offering	The worship
4	The sin offering	of Israel
5	(When sin offering is necessary) The trespass offering	
6	Rituals for burnt, cereal, sin,	
7	trespass, peace offerings; blood; priests' portion	
8	Consecration of Aaron, the priests, the tabernacle	
9	Consecration ceremonies	The priesthood
10	Nadab and Abihu	
11	Clean, unclean animals	
12	Women after childbirth	
13	Leprosy: Diagnosis,	Laws of
14	treatment; leprosy in houses	purity
15	Sexual uncleanness	
16	The Scapegoat	Atonement ritual
17	Laws for killing animals	
18	Laws for sexual relations	
19	Laws for behavior	
20	Laws against pagan behavior	
21	Laws about priesthood	The Holiness Code
22	and sacrifices	
23	The Liturgical Year	
24	Other rules	
25	Sabbatical year	
26	P's exhortation	
27	Miscellaneous material	Appendix

NUMBERS

1	The census	
2	Arrangement of tribes marching, camping	
3	The Levites:	
4	Kohathites, Gershonites, Merarites; census	The census in the
5	Laws and rules	wilderness of Sinai
6	Nazirites	
7	Offerings	
8	Gold lampstand; Levites	
9	Passover	
10	Leaving the Sinai Wilderness	
11	Complaints about manna; quails provided	On the move toward
12	Complaints against Moses by Aaron and Miriam	Paran
13	Twelve spies sent out	
14	Reports of spies disagree; minor invasion fails	
15	Various laws	
16	Rebellion of Korah, Dothan, and Abiram	The stay in
17	Aaron's rod sprouts	Paran
18	Priests and Levites	
19	Rite of the red heifer	
20	Miriam dies; waters of Meribah; Edom, Moab	From Kadesh
21	Hormah, bronze serpent, Sihon and Og defeated	To Moab
22	Balak sends for Balaam; Balaam's ass	
23	Oracles of Balaam	Balaam
24	Oracles of Balaam	
25	Unfaithfulness with Moab and Midian	
26	A second census	
27	Commission of Joshua	
28	Offerings: Daily, Sabbath, Unleavened Bread, Weeks	Laws and
29	Feast of Trumpets, Atonement, Booths	events
30	Women's vows	
31	Midianites destroyed	
32	Gad's, Reuben's, and Manasseh's settlement	
33	Route of the wandering	
34	Boundaries in Canaan	
35	Levitical cities, Cities of refuge	Appendix
36	Marriage Laws	

1	Moses reviews events of Sinai and Wandering	
2	The events in Transjordan	Moses' first address (1:1-4:43)
3	The events in Transjordan	
4	Danger of Idols	
5	The Ten Commandments	
6	"Hear O Israel..."	
7	Canaan must be conquered and destroyed	
8	"Man does not live by bread alone..."	
9	Moses reviews the incident of the Golden Calf	
10	Moses reviews the story of the tables of stone	
11	Israel's choice: Blessing or curse	
12	Worship is restricted to the place which the Lord will choose	
13	Shun idol worship	
14	Clean and unclean food; tithes	Moses' second address (4:43-28:68)
15	Year of release; debt slavery	
16	Passover; Weeks; Tabernacles	
17	Duties of Officials: Court, King,	
18	Priests; prophets	
19	Crimes	
20	Rules of War	
21	Various Laws	
22	Various Laws	
23	Various Laws	
24	Various Laws	
25	Various Laws	
26	First-fruits; "A wandering Aramean was my father..."	
27	Stones set up at Shechem; Blessing and cursing ceremony	
28	The blessings; the curses	
29	Sermon on the Covenant	Moses' third address (29:1-30:20)
30	"I set before you this day life and good, death and evil..."	
31	Moses takes his leave	
32	The Song of Moses	Appendix (31:1-34:12)
33	The Blessing of Moses	
34	Moses dies on Mount Nebo (Pisgah); Joshua takes command	

THE BOOK OF JOSHUA

1	Joshua becomes the leader of Israel		Introduction
2	Spies sent to Jericho		
3	Israel crosses the Jordan	The Gilgal story	Jericho
4	Twelve stones set up		
5	Israel encamps at Gilgal		
6	The fall of Jericho		
7	Israel defeated at Ai		Ai
8	Israel defeats Ai		
9	The Gibeonites deceive Joshua		Gibeon
10	The conquests in the South		Conquests
11	The conquests in the North		
12	Summary of conquests		
13	The land east of the Jordan		The division of the land
14	Caleb's inheritance		
15	Judah's territory		
16	Joseph's territory (Ephraim)		
17	Joseph's territory (Manasseh)		
18	Benjamin's territory		
19	Territory of Simeon, Zebulun, Issachar, Asher, Naphtali, Dan		
20	Cities of refuge designated		
21	Levitical cities designated		
22	The altar at the Jordan River		
23	Joshua's farewell address		
24	The Covenant at Shechem		Conclusion

THE BOOK OF JUDGES

1	Summary of the Conquest		Introduction
2	Introduction to period of the Judges		
3	Othniel, Ehud, Shamgar		
4	Prose version	Deborah	
5	Poetic version		
6	Gideon's call		
7	Gideon's victory	Gideon	Stories of Judges (2:6-16:31)
8	Gideon's refusal of kingship		
9	Abimelek becomes king		
10	Tola, Jair, Jephthah	Jephthah	
11	Jephthah's victory and vow		
12	Ibzan, Elon, Abdon		
13	Samson's birth		
14	Samson's marriage	Samson	
15	Samson slays Philistines		
16	Samson's betrayal by Delilah		
17	Micah obtains a Levite	Danite Story	
18	Dan moves to the north country		Appendices
19	The rape of the Levite's concubine	Story of Gibeah	
20	Punishment of the Benjaminites		
21	Peace is established		

THE BOOK OF RUTH

1	Ruth and Naomi go from Moab to Bethlehem	
2	Ruth gleans in Boaz's field	The story of David's ancestry
3	Ruth meets Boaz at the threshing floor	
4	Boaz marries Ruth	

THE FIRST BOOK OF SAMUEL

1	Birth and Dedication at Shiloh	
2	Song of Hannah; Eli's sons	Samuel as a child
3	Samuel's call	
4	Philistines capture the ark	
5	Troubles in Philistia	Story of the ark
6	Ark returned to Israel	
7	Samuel is judge	
8	The people ask for a king	
9	Saul seeks his father's asses	
10	Samuel anoints Saul king; Saul elected at Mizpah	Beginning of the monarchy
11	Saul aids Jabesh-Gilead; made king at Gilgal	
12	Samuel's farewell speech	
13	Samuel rebukes Saul at Gilgal	War against
14	Jonathan saved by the people	Philistines
15	Saul rejected by Samuel from being king	
16	David is anointed; David the lyre-player	David's
17	David and Goliath	rise
18	Saul's jealousy; David marries Michal	
19	David escapes from Saul	
20	David and Jonathan	
21	David at Nob and Gath	
22	Saul has Nob priests killed	
23	David at Keilah and Ziph	Saul vs.
24	David at Ein Gedi	David
25	David meets Abigail	
26	David spares Saul	
27	David dwells at Gath with King Achish	
28	Saul consults witch of Endor	
29	David not allowed to fight with Philistines	Saul's last
30	David raids Ziklag	battle
31	Saul dies on Mount Gilboa	

THE SECOND BOOK OF SAMUEL

1	David's lament over Saul and Jonathan	
2	David anointed king at Hebron; battle at pool of Gibeon	David king at Hebron
3	Abner quarrels with Ishbaal; Joab murders Abner	
4	Ishbaal murdered	
5	David captures Jerusalem, defeats Philistines	
6	Brings ark to Jerusalem	David king at Jerusalem
7	Nathan's prophecy	
8	Summary of David's deeds	
9	David and Mephibosheth	
10	The Ammonite War	David the man
11	The Bathsheba episode	
12	Nathan rebukes David	
13	Story of Amnon and Tamar; Absalom flees	
14	Parable of the Wise Woman	
15	Absalom rebels, David flees	
16	Ahithophel counsels Absalom	
17	Hushai's counsel is preferred	David's court
18	Absalom is killed	
19	David returns to Jerusalem by way of Gilgal	
20	Sheba leads a revolt	
21	The famine; David's soldiers	
22	Psalm of Thanksgiving	
23	The Testament of David; water from Bethlehem's well	Appendix
24	A census results in a plague	

THE FIRST BOOK OF THE KINGS

1	Solomon and Adonijah rivals for David's throne	} David's death
2	David dies; Solomon is king	
3	Solomon asks for wisdom; story of two harlots	
4	List of officials; Solomon's wealth and wisdom	
5	Preparation for new Temple	
6	Temple is built	
7	Other buildings, bronze altar, molten sea, lavers, etc.	} King Solomon
8	Dedication of the Temple	
9	Solomon's vision; other activities	
10	Visit of Queen of Sheba	
11	Solomon's idolatry; his death	
12	Ten tribes revolt; Jeroboam rebuilds Shechem	
13	Man of God at Bethel	
14	Jeroboam dies; Rehoboam's reign; Shishak's invasion	
15	Abijam; Asa; war between Asa and Baasha; Nadab	
16	Elah; civil war; Omri; Ahab	
17	Elijah is fed by ravens	
18	Elijah and Baal prophets on Mt. Carmel	
19	Elijah at Horeb--"still small voice"	Stories of Elijah and Elisha
20	Ahab and the Syrians	The Kingdoms of Israel and Judah
21	Naboth's vineyard	
22	Ahab dies; Jehoshaphat; Ahaziah	

Israel

Judah

1	Ahaziah		
2	Elijah taken by whirlwind; Elisha curses boys	Stories of Elijah and Elisha	The Kingdoms of Israel and Judah
3	Jehoram fights Moab		
4	Elisha's power illustrated		
5	Naaman healed, Gehazi punished		
6	Axhead floats; Syrians captured; Samaria sieged		
7	End of Samaria's siege		
8	Elisha and Hazael; Jehoram; Ahaziah		
9	Jehu; Jezebel		
10	Jehu kills Ahab's family, Baal worshippers		
11	Athaliah the queen		
12	Jehoash		
13	Jehoahaz, Elisha's death		
14	Amaziah; Jereboam 11		
15	Azariah; Zechariah; Shallum; Menahem, Pekahiah, Pekah, Jotham		
16	Ahaz; Syro-Ephraimite War		
17	Hoshea; Deuteronomic sermon; Samaritans; the end of Northern Kingdom		
18	Hezekiah; Samaria falls; Sennacherib; Hezekiah is delivered		
19	Jerusalem is saved		
20	Hezekiah's sickness		
21	Manasseh; Amon	The Kingdom of Judah	
22	Josiah; law book discovered		
23	Covenant made; reform begun; Jehoahaz; Jehoiakim		
24	Jehoiakin, Zedekiah		
25	Jerusalem destroyed; Gedaliah is governor		

THE FIRST BOOK OF THE CHRONICLES

1	Genealogy from Adam to Israel	
2	Judah's descendants	
3	David's descendants	
4	Judah's and Simeon's descendants	
5	Descendants of the Tribes in Transjordan	Genealogies
6	The descendants of Levi	
7	The descendants of the Northern Tribes	
8	Descendants of Benjamin	
9	The families of Jerusalem	
10	Saul's reign and death	
11	David becomes king in Hebron	
12	" " " " "	
13	Story of the ark	
14	David in Jerusalem	
15	More about the ark	
16	Psalm of Thanksgiving	
17	David wishes to build a Temple	
18	Military victories	
19	" "	David
20	" "	
21	Census results in a plague	
22	David prepares for Solomon to build the Temple	
23	About the Levites	
24	" " "	
25	" " "	
26	" " "	
27	Administrative lists	
28	David's speech	
29	" " , David dies	

THE SECOND BOOK OF THE CHRONICLES

1	Solomon is king; his wisdom
2	The building of the Temple
3	" " " " "
4	" " " " "
5	The Temple is consecrated
6	" " " "
7	" " " "
8	Solomon's other activities
9	Queen of Sheba visits
10	Rehoboam
11	"
12	"
13	Abijah
14	Asa
15	"
16	"
17	Jehoshaphat
18	"
19	"
20	"
21	Jehoram
22	Ahaziah
23	Athaliah
24	Joash
25	Amaziah
26	Uzziah
27	Jotham
28	Ahaz
29	Hezekiah; cleanses the temple
30	The Passover
31	His reforms
32	Assyrians invade; Hezekiah dies
33	Manasseh, Amon
34	Josiah
35	Death of Josiah
36	Other Judean kings

Solomon

Judean kings

THE BOOK OF EZRA

1	Edict of Cyrus	⎫ Sheshbazzar's return
2	List of those returning	⎭
3	Zerubbabel and Jeshua rebuild altar	⎫
4	Trouble with Samaritans	⎪
5	Report sent to Darius	⎬ Temple built under Darius
6	Darius' answer; Temple finished	⎭
7	Ezra returns	⎫ Ezra's return
8	Others return with Ezra	⎭
9	Problem of mixed marriages	⎫ Mixed marriages
10	The solution of the problem	⎭

THE BOOK OF NEHEMIAH

1	Nehemiah's prayer	⎫
2	Requests permission to go to Jerusalem; arrives	⎪
3	Walls are rebuilt	⎪
4	The antagonism of the neighbors	⎬ Nehemiah's memoirs
5	Financial problems	⎪
6	Walls completed	⎪
7	List of exiles who returned	⎭
8	The Law is read; Booths celebrated	⎫
9	Ezra's speech	⎪
10	The written agreement	⎬ The Ezra story
11	Where they lived	⎭
12	Dedication of the walls	⎫ Nehemiah's memoirs
13	Nehemiah's reforms	⎭

ESTHER

1	Queen Vashti refuses to come before King Ahasuerus	Esther becomes queen
2	Esther is chosen to replace Vashti	
3	Haman arranges for a pogrom	Esther, the King, Mordecai and Haman
4	Mordecai persuades Esther to intercede	
5	Esther entertains the king and Haman at a banquet	
6	The king requires Haman to honor Mordecai	
7	Haman's plan is revealed; he is hanged	
8	Esther obtains another decree from the king	
9	Origin of Purim	The Feast of Purim
10	Mordecai is praised	

JOB

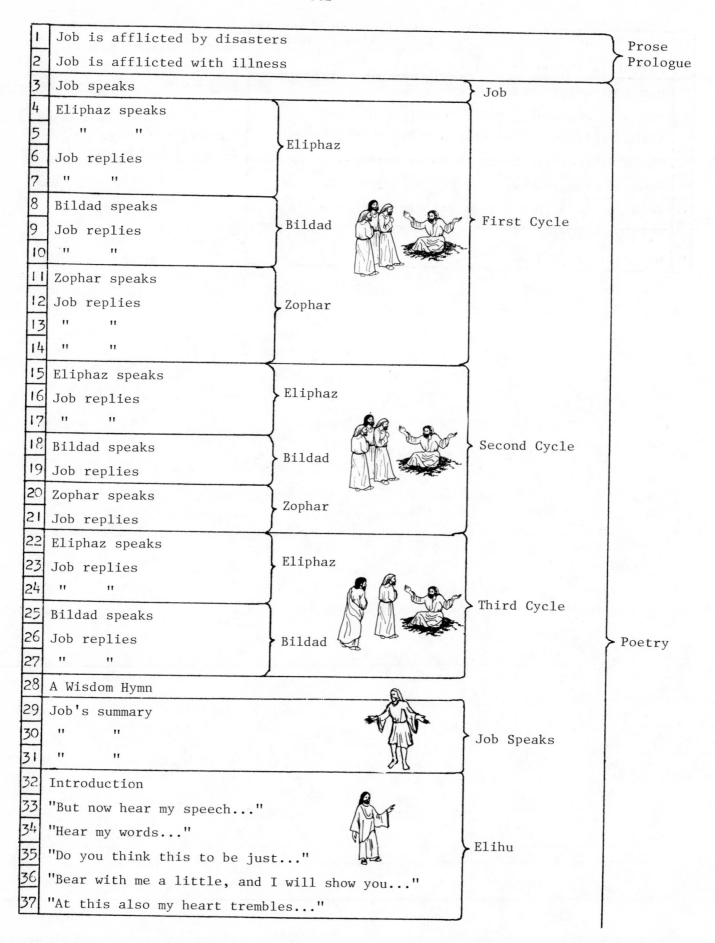

1	Job is afflicted by disasters		Prose Prologue
2	Job is afflicted with illness		
3	Job speaks	Job	
4	Eliphaz speaks	Eliphaz	First Cycle
5	" "		
6	Job replies		
7	" "		
8	Bildad speaks	Bildad	
9	Job replies		
10	" "		
11	Zophar speaks	Zophar	
12	Job replies		
13	" "		
14	" "		
15	Eliphaz speaks	Eliphaz	Second Cycle
16	Job replies		
17	" "		
18	Bildad speaks	Bildad	
19	Job replies		
20	Zophar speaks	Zophar	
21	Job replies		
22	Eliphaz speaks	Eliphaz	Third Cycle
23	Job replies		
24	" "		
25	Bildad speaks	Bildad	
26	Job replies		
27	" "		
28	A Wisdom Hymn		
29	Job's summary	Job Speaks	
30	" "		
31	" "		
32	Introduction	Elihu	
33	"But now hear my speech..."		
34	"Hear my words..."		
35	"Do you think this to be just..."		
36	"Bear with me a little, and I will show you..."		
37	"At this also my heart trembles..."		

Poetry

38	Job is answered from the whirlwind		
39	" " " " " "	יהוה	God's Answer
40	" " " " " "		
41	" " " " " "		
42	Prose Epilogue		Prose Epilogue

21

1	"Blessed is the man who walks not in the counsel of the wicked..."
2	"Why do the nations conspire and the peoples plot in vain?..."
3	"O Lord, how many are my foes..."
4	"Answer me when I call, O God of my right..."
5	"Give ear to my words, O Lord..."
6	"O Lord, rebuke me not in thy anger..."
7	"O Lord, my God, in theé do I take refuge..."
8	"O Lord, our God, how majestic is thy name in all the earth..."
9	"I will give thanks to the Lord with my whole heart..."
10	"Why dost thou stand afar off, O Lord?..."
11	"In the Lord I take my refuge..."
12	"Help, Lord, for there is no longer any that is godly..."
13	"How long, O Lord? Wilt thou forget me for ever?..."
14	"The fool says in his heart, 'There is no God'..."
15	"O Lord, who shall sojourn in thy tent?..."
16	"Preserve me, O God, for in thee I take refuge..."
17	"Hear a just cause, O Lord; attend to my cry..."
18	"I love thee, O Lord, my strength..."
19	"The heavens are telling the glory of God..."
20	"The Lord answer you in the day of trouble..."
21	"In thy strength the king rejoices, O Lord..."
22	"My God, my God, why hast thou forsaken me?..."
23	"The Lord is my shepherd, I shall not want..."
24	"The earth is the Lord's and the fullness thereof..."
25	"To thee, O Lord, I lift up my soul..."
26	"Vindicate me, O Lord, for I have walked in my integrity..."
27	"The Lord is my light and my salvation; whom shall I fear?..."
28	"To thee, O Lord, I call; my rock, be not deaf to me..."
29	"Ascribe to the Lord, O heavenly beings, ascribe to the Lord..."
30	"I will extol thee, O Lord, for thou hast drawn me up..."
31	"In thee, O Lord, do I seek refuge..."
32	"Blessed is he whose transgression is forgiven..."
33	"Rejoice in the Lord, O you righteous!..."
34	"I will bless the Lord at all times..."
35	"Contend, O Lord, with those who contend with me..."
36	"Transgression speaks to the wicked deep in his heart..."
37	"Fret not yourself because of the wicked..."
38	"O Lord, rebuke me not in thy anger..."
39	"I said, 'I will guard my ways that I sin not with my tongue'..."
40	"I waited patiently for the Lord..."
41	"Blessed is he who considers the poor..."

42	"As a hart longs for flowing streams, so longs my soul..."
43	"Vindicate me, O God, and defend my cause..."
44	"We have heard with our ears, O God, our fathers have told us..."
45	"My heart overflows with a goodly theme..."
46	"God is our refuge and strength, a very present help in trouble..."
47	"Clap your hands, all peoples. Shout to God with loud songs of joy..."
48	"Great is the Lord and greatly to be praised in the city of our God!..."
49	"Hear this, all peoples! Give ear, all inhabitants of the world..."
50	"The mighty one, God the Lord, speaks and summons the earth..."
51	"Have mercy on me, O God, according to thy steadfast love..."
52	"Why do you boast, O mighty man, of mischief done against the godly?..."
53	"The fool says in his heart, 'There is no God'..."
54	"Save me, O God, by thy name, and vindicate me by thy might..."
55	"Give ear to my prayers, O God; and hide not thyself from my supplication..."
56	"Be gracious to me, O God, for men trample upon me..."
57	"Be merciful to me, O God, be merciful to me..."
58	"Do you indeed decree what is right, you gods?..."
59	"Deliver me from my enemies, O my God..."
60	"O God, thou hast rejected us, broken our defenses..."
61	"Hear my cry, O God, listen to my prayer..."
62	"For God alone my soul waits in silence..."
63	"O God, thou art my God, I seek thee, my soul thirsts for thee..."
64	"Hear my voice, O God, in my complaint..."
65	"Praise is due to thee, O God, in Zion..."
66	"Make a joyful noise to God, all the earth..."
67	"May God be gracious to us and bless..."
68	"Let God arise, let his enemies be scattered..."
69	"Save me, O God! For the waters have come up to my neck..."
70	"Be pleased, O God, to deliver me!..."
71	"In thee, O Lord, do I take refuge..."
72	"Give the king thy justice, O God, and thy righteousness to the royal son..."

144	"Blessed be the Lord, my rock..."
145	"I will extol thee, my God and King..."
146	"Praise the Lord! Praise the Lord, O my soul!..."
147	"Praise the Lord! For it is a good thing to sing praises to our God..."
148	"Praise the Lord! Praise the Lord from the heavens..."
149	"Praise the Lord! Sing to the Lord a new song..."
150	"Praise the Lord! Praise God in his sanctuary..."

1	"The fear of the Lord is the beginning of knowledge..."	
2	"For the Lord gives wisdom..."	The
3	"The Lord by wisdom founded the earth..."	Praise
4	"Let your heart hold fast my words..."	of
5	"Drink water from your own cistern..."	Wisdom
6	"Go to the ant, O sluggard; consider her ways..."	
7	"Say to wisdom, 'You are my sister'..."	
8	"The Lord created me at the beginning of his work..."	
9	"Wisdom has built her house..."	
10	"A wise son makes a glad father..."	
11	"A false balance is an abomination to the Lord..."	
12	"Whoever loves discipline loves knowledge..."	
13	"He who spares the rod hates his son..."	
14	"The simple believes everything..."	
15	"A soft answer turns away wrath..."	
16	"Pride goes before destruction..."	
17	"He who restrains his words has knowledge..."	
18	"The words of a man's mouth are deep waters..."	
19	"A wife's quarreling is a continual dripping of rain..."	Short
20	"He who goes about gossiping reveals secrets..."	Proverbs
21	"It is better to live in a corner...than...with a contentious woman..."	
22	"Incline your ear, and hear the words of the wise..."	
23	"When you sit down to eat with a ruler..."	
24	"A little sleep, a little slumber..."	
25	"Let your foot be seldom in your neighbor's house..."	
26	"He who meddles in a quarrel not his own..."	
27	"Do not boast about tomorrow..."	
28	"The wicked flee when no one pursues..."	
29	"The rod and reproof give wisdom..."	
30	"Three things are too wonderful for me..."	Words of Agur
31	"A good wife who can find?..."	Good Wife

ECCLESIASTES

1	"Vanity of vanities," says the Preacher..."all is vanity..."	World Outlook
2	"Come now, I will make a test of pleasure..."	
3	"A time to be born, a time to die..."	
4	"This also is vanity and a striving after wind..."	The Experience of the Wise Man
5	"When dreams increase, empty words grow many..."	
6	"Who knows what is good for man?..."	
7	"Be not righteous overmuch, and do not make yourself overwise..."	
8	"Who is like the wise man?..."	
9	"A living dog is better than a dead lion..."	
10	"He who digs a pit will fall into it..."	Advice
11	"Cast your bread upon the waters..."	
12	"Before the silver cord is snapped, or the golden bowl is broken..."	

SONG OF SOLOMON

1	"O that you would kiss me with the kisses of your mouth..."
2	"I am a rose of Sharon, a lily of the valleys..."
3	"Upon my bed by night I sought him whom my soul loves..."
4	"Behold, you are beautiful, my love..."
5	"I come to my garden, my sister, my bride..."
6	"I am my beloved's and my beloved is mine..."
7	"How graceful are your feet in sandals..."
8	"My vineyard, my very own, is for myself..."

1	"Come now let us reason together, says the Lord..."	
2	"For out of Zion shall go forth the law..."	
3	"The daughters of Zion are haughty..."	
4	"The branch of the Lord shall be beautiful..."	
5	"Let me sing for my beloved a love song..."	Oracles concerning Israel and Judah
6	"In the year that King Uzziah died..."	
7	"Behold, a young woman shall conceive..."	
8	"This people have refused the waters of Shiloah..."	
9	"For unto us a child is born..."	
10	"Ah, Assyria, the rod of my anger..."	
11	"There shall come forth a shoot..."	
12	"You will draw water from the wells of salvation..."	
13	"On a bare hill raise a signal..."	
14	"As I have planned, so shall it be..."	
15	"The daughter of Dibon has gone up..."	
16	"A throne will be established in steadfast love..."	
17	"Behold, Damascus will cease to be a city..."	Oracles against Foreign Nations
18	"When a signal is raised on the mountains, look..."	
19	"The waters of the Nile will be dried up..."	
20	"As my servant Isaiah has walked naked and barefoot..."	
21	"As whirlwinds in the Negeb sweep on..."	
22	"You made a reservoir between the two walls..."	
23	"The oracle concerning Tyre..."	
24	"Then the moon will be confounded..."	
25	"A feast of fat things..."	Isaiah Apocalypse
26	"Thou dost keep him in perfect peace..."	
27	"The Lord...will punish Leviathan..."	
28	"The priest and prophet reel with strong drink..."	
29	"As when a thirsty man dreams he is drinking..."	Oracles concerning Israel and Judah (705-701 BC)
30	"Woe to the rebellious children..."	
31	"Woe to those who go down to Egypt for help..."	
32	"Like...the shade of a great rock in a weary land..."	
33	"Jerusalem, a quiet habitation, an immovable tent..."	
34	"Draw near, O nation, to hear, and hearken, O peoples!..."	Oracles from Exilic times
35	"The desert shall rejoice and blossom..."	
36	"Sennacherib...came up against all the fortified cities..."	
37	"Then Sennacherib king of Assyria departed..."	Historical Appendix (see 2 Ki. 18: 13-20:19)
38	"In those days Hezekiah became sick..."	
39	"Merodach-Baladan...sent envoys with letters...to Hezekiah..."	

40	"Comfort, comfort my people, says your God..."	
41	"Who stirred up one from the east?..."	
42	"Behold my servant, whom I uphold..."	
43	"Behold, I am doing a new thing..:"	Before the
44	"All who make idols are nothing..."	Fall of
45	"Thus says the Lord to his anointed, to Cyrus..."	Babylon
46	"Bel bows down, Nebo stoops..."	
47	"Come and sit in the dust, O virgin daughter of Babylon..."	
48	"The former things I have declared of old..."	
49	"Listen to me, O coastlands..."	
50	"The Lord God has given me a tongue..."	
51	"Hearken to me, you who pursue deliverance..."	After the
52	"Behold my servant shall prosper..."	Fall of
53	"Who has believed what we have heard?..."	Babylon
54	"Sing, O barren one, who did not bear..."	
55	"Ho, everyone who thirsts, come to the waters..."	
56	"My house shall be called a house of prayer..."	
57	"I dwell...with him who is of a contrite and humble spirit..."	
58	"Is not this the fast I choose: to loose the bonds..."	
59	"He put on righteousness as a breastplate..."	
60	"Arise, shine, for your light has come..."	
61	"The Spirit of the Lord God is upon me because the Lord..."	
62	"You shall no more be termed Forsaken..."	
63	"Why is thy apparel red...like his that treads the wine press?..."	
64	"We are the clay, and thou art our potter..."	
65	"The wolf and the lamb shall feed together..."	
66	"Heaven is my throne and the earth is my footstool..."	

II
ISAIAH

III?
ISAIAH

JEREMIAH

1	Jeremiah's inaugural visions	
2	Israel is apostate	
3	Judah is worse than Israel	
4	Judah is threatened with invasion	
5	Judah's sin	
6	Judgment is coming	
7	The Temple Sermon of Jeremiah	
8	Is there no balm in Gilead?	
9	Lament for Judah and Jerusalem	
10	God will overthrow idols	
11	The Covenant is proclaimed	Oracles of Jeremiah
12	The complaint of Jeremiah	
13	The linen waistcloth	
14	Judah is to be punished	
15	Jeremiah complains	
16	Jeremiah forbidden to marry	
17	Judah's sin	
18	The allegory of the potter	
19	The broken flask	
20	Jeremiah put in stocks	
21	Oracles concerning Zedekiah	From Time of Zedekiah
22	" " Jehoahaz, Jehoiakim, Jehoiakin	
23	Woe to the shepherds	
24	Vision of the baskets of figs	
25	Babylon will punish Judah	
26	The Temple Sermon	
27	The yoke of Babylon	
28	The yoke of Babylon	
29	Jeremiah writes to the Exiles	Part I (mostly memoirs from Baruch)
30	Book of Consolation	
31	Book of Consolation	
32	Jeremiah purchases land	
33	Appendix to Book of Consolation	
34	Slaves released	
35	The Rechabites	

36	Jeremiah's scroll read to Jehoiakim		
37	The siege under Zedekiah		
38	The siege under Zedekiah		Biography of Jeremiah
39	The Fall of Jerusalem		
40	The third revolt	Part II Jeremiah's suffering	
41	Gedaliah murdered		
42	Jeremiah flees to Egypt		
43	In Egypt		
44	" "		
45	" "		
46	Against Egypt		
47	Against Philistia		
48	Against Moab		Oracles against Foreign Nations
49	Against Ammon, Edom, Damascus, etc.		
50	Against Babylon		
51	" "		
52	(Duplicates 2 Ki. 24:18-25:30)		Historical appendix

LAMENTATIONS

1	Jerusalem is a widow
2	The people suffer
3	Personal lament
4	Siege and destruction of Jerusalem
5	A psalm of lament

EZEKIEL

1	Ezekiel's inaugural vision	
2	Ezekiel eats the scroll	
3	Commissioned to be a watchman	
4	Siege of Jerusalem symbolized	
5	Cuts hair symbolically	
6	High Places will be destroyed	
7	The end is come upon you	
8	Idolatry in the Temple	Visit
9	The guilty will be killed	to
10	God's Glory departs	Temple
11	Hope for the Exiles	
12	Symbol of the Exile in packed baggage	
13	Against false prophets and prophetesses	
14	The righteous can only save themselves	
15	The vine is a symbol for the people of Jerusalem	
16	Israel is like an unfaithful wife	
17	The two eagles and the cedar	
18	The fathers have eaten sour grapes	
19	The lioness and the vine	
20	The apostasy of Israel	
21	Prophecies about the sword	
22	Condemnation of Jerusalem	
23	Oholah and Oholibah, unfaithful wives	
24	Death of Ezekiel's wife	

Denunciations of
Judah and Israel
(593-588 BC)

25	Against foreign nations	
26	Against Tyre	Oracles
27	" "	against
28	" " and Sidon	Tyre & Sidon
29	The Pharaoh	Oracles
30	Destruction of Egypt	against
31	Egypt, the great cedar	Egypt
32	Lamentations over Pharaoh	

Denunciations of
Foreign Nations
(587-571 BC)

33

33	Responsibility		
34	The shepherds and their sheep		
35	Mount Seir		
36	Mountains of Israel and people restored		
37	Valley of Dry Bones		
38	Oracles about Gog	Gog from Magog	
39	Gog's hordes destroyed		
40	Description of Temple		
41	Description of Temple		
42	Description of Temple	Vision of Israel Restored in Jerusalem	
43	Return of God's Glory		
44	Ordinances of the Temple		
45	" " " "		
46	" " " "		
47	River flowing from Temple		
48	Boundaries of the Land		

Future Restoration
of Israel
(585-573 BC)

DANIEL

1	Daniel and companions	
2	Dream of Nebuchadnezzar	
3	Three young men in furnace of fire	Stories of Deliverance
4	Nebuchadnezzar becomes mad	
5	The banquet of Belshazzar	
6	Daniel in the lion's den	
7	The vision of four beasts	
8	The vision of a ram and a he-goat	
9	The prophecy of seventy weeks	Apocalyptic "prophecies"
10	Prologue	The Vision of the Last Days
11	The vision	
12	Epilogue	

HOSEA

1	Hosea marries Gomer, the prostitute	Hosea and his unfaithful wife
2	Israel is like a harlot	
3	Gomer is taken back	
4	"The Lord has a controversy..."	
5	"When Ephraim saw his sickness..."	
6	"I desire steadfast love and not sacrifice..."	
7	"Ephraim is like a dove, silly and without sense..."	
8	"For they sow the wind, and they shall reap the whirlwind..."	God judges Israel
9	"Ephraim is stricken, their root is dried up..."	
10	"You have plowed iniquity, you have reaped injustice..."	
11	"When Israel was a child, I loved him..."	
12	"A trader, in whose hands are false balances..."	
13	"Men kiss calves!..."	
14	"O Ephraim, what have I to do with idols?..."	

JOEL

1	The locust plague
2	The locusts attack
3	The final battle and day of judgment

AMOS

1	Of Damascus, Philistia, Tyre, Edom, Ammon	} Condemnations
2	Of Moab, Judah, Israel	
3	The Chosen People have responsibilities	
4	Israel's extravagant piety	} Israel will be punished
5	The punishment of Israel	
6	Luxurious living seems to indicate security	
7	Locusts, Fire, Plumb Line	
8	Basket of summer fruit	} Visions
9	The Lord at the altar, Booth of David	

OBADIAH

1	Prophecy against Edom

JONAH

1	Jonah is commissioned to preach to Nineveh
2	A psalm used as a prayer of Jonah
3	Jonah in Nineveh
4	Jonah's anger over the repentance of Nineveh

36

MICAH

1	"What is the transgression of Jacob?..."	⎫
2	"They covet fields and sieze them..."	⎬ Samaria and Jerusalem threatened
3	"Zion shall be plowed as a field..."	⎭
4	Mountain of the House of the Lord	⎫
5	Bethlehem Ephrathah	⎬ The hope of Israel's future
6	Threats against Israel	
7	Hopeful prophecies for Israel	

NAHUM

1	"His way is in the whirlwind and storm..."	⎫ Poem: the power of Yahweh
2	"Nineveh is like a pool whose waters run away..."	⎫ The Fall of Nineveh
3	"Wasted is Nineveh; who will bemoan her?..."	⎭

HABAKKUK

1	"Why dost thou look on faithless men?..."	⎫ Oracles
2	"The righteous shall live by his faith..."	⎭
3	Habakkuk's Prayer	⎬ A Psalm

ZEPHANIAH

1	"A day of wrath is that day, a day of distress and anguish..."
2	"Come together and hold assembly, O shameless nation..."
3	"Woe to her that is rebellious and defiled..."

HAGGAI

1	"Is it a time for you yourselves to dwell in your panelled houses?..."
2	"The latter splendor of this house shall be greater than the former..."

ZECHARIAH

1	"I saw in the night...a man riding upon a red horse..."	
2	"Behold, a man with a measuring line in his hand..."	
3	"Then he showed me Joshua...and Satan standing at his right hand..."	
4	"Behold, a lampstand all of gold..."	520-518 BC
5	"Behold a flying scroll..."	
6	"Behold, four chariots..."	
7	"Render true judgments..."	
8	"Ten men from the nations...shall take hold of the robe of a Jew..."	
9	"Lo, your king comes to you...humble, riding on an ass..."	
10	"Ask rain from the Lord..."	
11	"I took two staffs; one I named Grace; the other I named Union..."	4th and 3rd Cent. BC
12	"And I will pour out on the house of David..."	
13	"Strike the shepherd that the sheep may be scattered..."	
14	"On that day living waters shall flow out from Jerusalem..."	

MALACHI

1	"I have loved you," says the Lord...
2	"Have we not all one father?..."
3	"Behold, I send my messenger to prepare the way before me..."
4	"Behold, I will send you Elijah the prophet before the...day of the Lord come..."

VISUAL OUTLINES
OF THE
APOCRYPHA

THE FIRST BOOK OF ESDRAS

("Esdras α" in LXX; "Esdras III" in Vulgate)

1	From Josiah to the Babylonian Exile	(cf. 2 Chron. 35:1–36:21)
2	From Cyrus' decree to Zerubbabel	(cf. Ezra 1:1-11)
3	"Wine is strongest."	Story of the 3 bodyguards
4	"The king...women...truth is strongest."	
5	List of returnees; Temple construction starts.	
6	Darius' decree is confirmed.	Jews return with Zerubbabel,
7	Completion of the Temple.	rebuild Temple, proclaim
8	Ezra's proclamation of the Law.	Law

THE SECOND BOOK OF ESDRAS

1	Ezra announces God's rejection of the Jews		Chris-	Esdras V
2	God is Father, Mother, Nurse.		tian	in Vulgate
3				
4	The anguish of God's people.	First		
5				
6	God's punishment of his people.	Second		
7				
8	7-day judgment; then 400-year period.	Third	Visions	Esdras IV
9				in Vulgate
10	Ezra's vision of the mourning woman.	Fourth		
11	The vision of the eagle from the sea.	Fifth		
12				
13	The vision of the "Son of God" from the sea.	Sixth		
14	Ezra re-writes the Law after it is burnt.	Seventh		
15	The righteous will be brought out of Egypt; disasters follow.		Words of	Esdras VI
16	Great destruction and confusion for sinners; hope for faithful.		the Lord	in Vulgate

TOBIT

1	In Nineveh Tobit is punished for his religious beliefs.	
2	Tobit is blinded by sparrow's dung.	
3	Tobit and a young woman, Sarah, both pray for death.	
4	Tobit's son, Tobias, goes to collect his father's money.	
5	The angel Raphael accompanies Tobias	Story of
6	Tobias takes gall, heart, and liver from a fish. Told to marry Sarah.	Tobit
7	Tobias marries Sarah.	
8	Tobias exorcizes the demon with the heart and liver of the fish.	
9	Tobias sends Raphael for the money.	
10	Tobias hurries toward home after the marriage festival.	
11	He heals his father's eyes with the gall of the fish.	
12	Raphael reveals his true identity.	
13	A "Prayer of Rejoicing" by Tobit.	
14	Tobit's exhortation.	

JUDITH

1	Nebuchadnezzar asks help for his war against the king of the Medes.	
2	Help is refused and Holofernes sent to punish those who refuse.	
3	Tyre, Sidon, Azotus, and Ascalon capitulate.	Historical
4	The Jews prepare their defences against Holofernes and pray.	setting of
5	Achior, the Ammonite, explains that God protects Jews unless they sin.	story
6	Achior sent to Bethulia to suffer in the attack on the Jews.	
7	Holofernes cuts off water supply of Bethulia.	
8	Judith, a devout widow, devises a plan of deliverance.	
9	Judith prays to God concerning her plan.	
10	She dresses herself attractively and goes to Holofernes with her maid.	
11	She tells him God plans to punish the Jews and she will find out when.	Story of
12	Holofernes gets drunk at a banquet.	Judith
13	Judith cuts off his head and carries it out of the camp with her maid.	
14	The head is hung on the wall and panic ensues.	
15	The Jews drive off the army. Judith is awarded.	
16	Hymn of Thanksgiving. Judith dedicates her awards to God.	

THE ADDITIONS TO THE BOOK OF ESTHER
(in the order of the Septuagint Version but
with the chapter numbers of the King James Version)

11:2	Mordecai's dream of two dragons.
12	He discovers an assassination plot against the king.
	Esther 1:1--3:13 follows in the Septuagint.
13:1-7	A copy of the letter described in 3:13.
	Esther 3:14--4:17 follows in the Septuagint.
13:8-18	Mordecai's Prayer.
14	Esther's Prayer
15	Esther enters before the king and faints.
	Esther 5:3--8:12 follows in the Septuagint.
16	A copy of Artaxerxes' letter.
	Esther 8:13--10:3 follows in the Septuagint.
	(The Hebrew Esther ends here, but the Septuagint adds the following material.)
10:4-13	Mordecai's final speech
11:1	Addendum about the letter concerning Purim.

THE WISDOM OF SOLOMON

1	Wisdom leads to the reward of immortality.	
2	Refutation of philosophy of "living for the moment."	
3	The righteous have hope of immortality; the ungodly are punished.	Wisdom in daily life
4	Virtue leads to immortality.	
5	The ungodly have no hope like the righteous have.	
6	An appeal to those in authority to be instructed about Wisdom.	
7	Solomon describes Wisdom as a cosmic principle.	
8	He sought to marry Wisdom.	Divine Wisdom
9	Prayer that Wisdom may be given to him.	
10	Wisdom from Creation to the Exodus.	
11	At the Wandering in the Wilderness.	
12	The folly of the practices of the Canaanites.	
13	Idol worshippers are foolish.	
14	" " " "	Wisdom versus Folly in History
15	" " " "	
16	The worshippers of animals are foolish.	
17	God judges those of darkness.	
18	The pillar of fire and the death of the first-born.	
19	The new creation which obeys God.	

חָכְמָה

ECCLESIASTICUS, OR
THE WISDOM OF JESUS THE SON OF SIRACH

44	"Let us now praise famous men..."
45	"From his descendants the Lord brought forth..."
46	"Joshua the son of Nun was mighty in war..."
47	"After him Nathan rose up to prophesy..."
48	"Then the prophet Elijah arose like a fire..."
49	"The memory of Josiah is like a blending of incense..."
50	"The leader of his brethren ..was Simon the high priest..."
51	Epilogue

BARUCH

1	"...the time when the Chaldeans took Jerusalem and burnt it..."	Prose section
2	The Jews confess their sin.	
3	The fountain of Wisdom.	Poetic section
4		
5	"Take off the garment of your sorrow and affliction..."	Lament of Jerusalem

THE LETTER OF JEREMIAH

Warning against idol worship.

THE PRAYER OF AZARIAH
AND THE SONG OF THE THREE YOUNG MEN

"Blessed art thou, O Lord, God of our fathers..."

SUSANNA

Susanna's attempted seducers are proved guilty.

BEL AND THE DRAGON

☐ Daniel proves that Bel does not consume its offerings. Destroys dragon.

THE PRAYER OF MANASSEH

☐ "O Lord Almighty, God of our fathers..."

THE FIRST BOOK OF THE MACCABEES

1	Antiochus Epiphanes demands that Jews keep Greek customs.		Beginnings
2	Mattathias starts a revolt; Judas appointed leader.		of revolt
3	Judas' first victories.	Early Phase	
4	The Temple is rededicated and fortified.		
5	Battles in Galilee, Gilead, Judea.		Judas
6	Battles in Jerusalem.	Middle Phase	Maccabeus
7	Alcimus reinstated as High Priest.		
8	Treaty with Rome; Judas killed at Berea.	Last Phase	
9	Jonathan defeats Bacchides. Defeats Appollonius.		
10			
11	Jonathan's alliances.		Jonathan
12	Jonathan captured.		Maccabeus
13	Simon captures Gazara and Jerusalem's citadel.		
14	Simon's high priesthood made heriditary (Hasmonean).		Simon
15	Simon given right to coin money in his own name.		Maccabeus
16	Simon's son, John, becomes his successor.		

1	First letter to Jews in Egypt.	Letters and
2	Second letter to Jews in Egypt. Prologue to the history.	Prologue
3	Seleucus and Heliodorus fail to get money in Temple raid.	Jewish
4	Menelaus buys the high priesthood for himself.	Wrongdoings
5	Antiochus restores Menelaus to high priesthood; Judas Maccabeus flees.	Compulsory
6	Martyrdom of two women, martyrdom of Eliazar.	Hellenization
7	Martyrdom of a mother and her seven sons.	
8	Judas' organization of the revolt.	
9	Antiochus Epiphanes dies.	
10	Temple recaptured and purified.	The Revolt
11	Lysias defeated at Bethzur. Letters are exchanged.	Under the
12	Additional battles.	Leadership of
13	Antiochus Eupator and Lysias all defeated.	Judas Maccábeus
14	Alcimus betrays Judas and Nicanor.	
15	Nicanor killed by Jews. Epilogue.	

VISUAL OUTLINES
OF THE
NEW TESTAMENT

The numbers at the left of the page indicate the chapter numbers.
The brackets indicate the major divisions of the books.

THE GOSPEL ACCORDING TO MATTHEW

1	Genealogy. Birth of Jesus.	Introduction
2	The Wise Men visit; flight to Egypt; slaughter of the innocents.	
3	John the Baptist baptizes Jesus.	
4	Jesus' temptation in the wilderness; the calling of first disciples.	
5	Beatitudes; "You have heard that it was said to the men of old..."	Sermon on Mount
6	"Beware of practicing your piety before men..."	
7	"Judge not, that you be not judged..."	
8	Healing of a leper, centurion's servant, Peter's mother-in-law, etc.	Narrative
9	Forgiveness; Matthew's call; Jesus and sinners; fasting; healings.	
10	The Twelve; their mission; what they must expect.	Twelve
11	John the Baptist inquires about Jesus; "Woe to you, Chorazin..."	Rejection
12	The Lord of the Sabbath heals on the Sabbath; A demoniac is healed.	
13	Parables concerning sowers and seeds, leaven, treasure, pearl, net.	Teaching
14	John Baptist executed; Feeding of 5000; Walking on water.	Narrative
15	What defiles a man? "Even the dogs eat the crumbs..."	
16	The leaven of Pharisees and Sadducees. "You are the Christ..."	
17	Transfiguration. Epileptic cured. The fish and the shekel.	
18	"Who is the greatest...? "How often shall...I forgive?"	Teaching
19	Divorce. "It is easier for a camel to go through the eye..."	Narrative
20	Laborers in the vineyard. "Whoever would be great among you..."	
21	Entry into Jerusalem. Money changers. Fig tree. "By what authority?"	
22	Parable of Marriage Feast. Taxes? Resurrection? The Great Command?	
23	"Whoever exalts himself..." "Woe to you..."	
24	Signs of the last days.	Teaching
25	Parable of 5 wise and 5 foolish Maidens, of Talents, of Sheep and Goats.	
26	Anointing. Judas' betrayal. Last Supper, Gethsemane. Arrest. Questioning.	Passion
27	Trial. Barabbas. Simon of Cyrene. Crucifixion. Death. Burial. Guard.	
28	Mary Magdalene. Jesus in Galilee. "Make disciples of all nations..."	Resurrection

MATTHEW

1	John the Baptist. Jesus' Baptism. First disciples. Healings.	
2	Paralytic. Levi. Fasting. "The Sabbath was made for man..."	
3	Withered hand. Crowds. The Twelve. Scribes. Mother and brothers.	
4	Parable of Sower; explanation. Parables of seeds. Storm. "Peace!"	Ministry of
5	The Gerasene demoniac. Jairus' daughter. Woman with issue of blood.	Teaching and
6	Nazareth. Mission of Twelve. Herod, John Baptist. Feeding of 5000.	Healing
7	Traditions concerning defilement. Syrophoenician woman. "Ephphatha"	
8	Feeding 4000. The leaven of Pharisees. "Trees walking." "Christ."	
9	Transfiguration. Epileptic boy. Greatest? "He that is not against us..."	
10	Divorce. Children. Rich young man. Rewards. James and John. Bartimaeus.	
11	Entry into Jerusalem. Fig Tree. Money Changers. "By what authority?"	In
12	Parable of vineyard and tenants. Taxes. Resurrection. Commandment.	Jerusalem
13	Prediction of Fall of Jerusalem, persecution, Son of Man. "Watch..."	
14	Anointing. Judas' betrayal. Last Supper. Gethsemane. Arrest. Denial.	The Passion
15	Trial. Barabbas. Simon of Cyrene. Crucifixion. Death. Burial.	
16	Mary Magdalene. Young man in white robe. "...for they were afraid..."	Resurrection

MARK

1	Annunciation to Zechariah, to Mary. Visit to Elizabeth. John born.	Birth and
2	Jesus' birth. Shepherds. Simeon. Jesus at twelve years.	Childhood
3	John the Baptist preaches. Jesus is baptized. Genealogy of Jesus.	
4	Temptation. Synagogues in Nazareth and Capernaum. Healings.	
5	Call of first disciples. Leper cleansed. Paralytic healed. Levi.	
6	Lord of Sabbath. Withered hand. Twelve chosen. Sermon on Plain.	
7	Centurion's servant healed. Widow's son. Jesus and John. Woman.	
8	Parable of sower. Storm. Gerasene demoniac. Jairus' daughter, woman.	
9	Mission of 12. Feeding 5000. Peter. Transfiguration. Exorcism.	
10	Mission of 70. Question of lawyer: Good Samaritan. Mary, Martha.	
11	Lord's Prayer. "Ask...seek..." Demons. Jonah. Woes.	
12	Warnings. Rich Fool. Treasure. Waiting Servants. Division.	Narrative of
13	Fig Tree. Healing on Sabbath. Mustard seed, leaven, narrow door.	Ministry
14	Healing on Sabbath. Parables of Banquets. Cost of discipleship.	
15	Parables of Lost Sheep, Lost Coin, Prodigal Son.	
16	Dishonest Steward. God and Mammon. Rich Man and Lazarus.	
17	Offending little ones. Unworthy servants. Lepers. Son of Man.	
18	Parables of Unjust Judge, Pharisee and tax collector, Rich Man, Blind Man.	
19	Zacchaeus. Parable of Pounds. Entry into Jerusalem and the Temple.	
20	By what authority? Parable of Tenants. Tribute to Caesar. Resurrection.	
21	Widow's offering. Impermanence of Temple. Son of Man. Fig Tree.	
22	Judas. Last Supper. Gethsemane. Arrest. Questioning.	Passion
23	Trial. Barabbas. Simon of Cyrene. Crucifixion. Death. Burial.	Narrative
24	Two men in white. On road to Emmaus. Appearance. Departure.	Resurrection

LUKE

1	Prologue. John the Baptist and his disciples witness.	Introduction
2	Marriage in Cana. Temple visited and cleansed.	
3	Visit of Nicodemus. "God so loved the world..." John testifies.	
4	Woman of Samaria and Jesus. Official's son healed.	
5	Jesus heals at Bethzatha on Sabbath. Jesus' discourse.	
6	Feeding of 5000. Storm on Sea of Galilee. Discourse on Bread of Heaven.	Narration of Ministry
7	Jesus teaches at Feast of Tabernacles. Attempt to arrest him.	
8	Woman taken in adultery. Light of World. Dialogue of Jesus and Jews.	
9	Jesus heals a man born blind.	
10	Parables of Sheepfold and Shepherd. Discourse at Feast of Dedication.	
11	Lazarus dies. He is raised. Jews plot against Jesus.	
12	Mary anoints Jesus. Entry into Jerusalem. Greeks seek him. Discourse.	
13	Maundy Thursday: washes disciples feet. Judas' departure.	
14	"In my Father's house are many rooms." "Yet a little while..."	Farewell Discourse
15	"I am the true vine..." "Love one another..." "If the world hates you..."	
16	The Counselor. "Ask, and you will receive..." "I have overcome..."	
17	Prayer for his disciples and for the Church.	High Priest
18	Gethsemane. Arrest. Questioning. Peter's denials. Trial. Barabbas.	Passion Narrative
19	Jesus is mocked. Cross carried. Crucifixion. Death. Burial.	
20	Mary Magdalene finds empty tomb. Jesus appears to her and to disciples.	Resurrection
21	Jesus appears at the Sea of Tiberias. "Feed my sheep."	

JOHN

THE SECOND LETTER OF PAUL TO THE CORINTHIANS

1 | Salutation. Thanksgiving. "I wanted to visit you on my way to Macedonia..."
2 | Paul goes to Macedonia to look for Titus.
3 | "You yourselves are our letter of recommendation." Moses' veil remains unlifted.
4 | "We preach not ourselves..." "treasure in earthen vessels..." "things unseen."
5 | "So we are ambassadors for Christ, God making his appeal through us."
6 | "Behold, now is the acceptable time; behold, now is the day of salvation.
7 | "For if I made you sorry with my letter, I do not regret it..."
8 | The generosity of the churches in Macedonia should be an example.
9 | "God loves a cheerful giver."
10 | "Let him who boasts, boast of the Lord."
11 | "Are they Hebrews? So am I. Are they Israelites? So am I."
12 | "To keep me from being too elated, a thorn was given me in the flesh..."
13 | "This is the third time I am coming to you." Exhortations. Greetings. Benediction.

THE LETTER OF PAUL TO THE GALATIANS

1 | Salutation. "The gospel which was preached by me is not man's gospel."
2 | "When Cephas came to Antioch I opposed him to the face..."
3 | "O foolish Galatians! Who has bewitched you...?" Faith, not works.
4 | "No longer a slave but a son..." "Abraham had two sons..."
5 | Christians are free. "If we live by the Spirit, let us walk by the Spirit."
6 | "Bear one another's burdens..." Summary.

THE LETTER OF PAUL TO THE EPHESIANS

1 | Salutation. "He has put all things under his feet, and has made him head..."
2 | "For he is our peace...and has broken down the dividing wall of hostility..."
3 | "I Paul, a prisoner for Christ Jesus on behalf of you Gentiles..."
4 | "There is one body and one Spirit, just as you were called to the one hope..."
5 | "Be subject to one another out of reverence for Christ."
6 | "Put on the whole armor of God..." Doxology.

THE LETTER OF PAUL TO THE PHILIPPIANS

1 | Salutation. "For to me to live is Christ, and to die is gain."
2 | "At the name of Jesus every knee should bow..."
3 | "Forgetting what lies behind and straining to what lies ahead, I press on..."
4 | "Finally, brethren, whatever is true, whatever is honorable..."

THE LETTER OF PAUL TO THE COLOSSIANS

|1| Salutation. "He is the image of the invisible God, the first-born of creation."
|2| "See to it that no one makes a prey of you by philosophy and empty deceit..."
|3| "If then you have been raised with Christ, seek the things that are above..."
|4| "Continue steadfastly in prayer..." Greetings to various people. The Grace.

THE FIRST LETTER OF PAUL TO THE THESSALONIANS

|1| Salutation. "We give thanks to God always for you all..."
|2| "For you yourselves know, brethren, that our visit to you was not in vain..."
|3| "Therefore...we were willing to be left behind at Athens alone..."
|4| "We would not have you ignorant, brethren, concerning those who are asleep..."
|5| "You are all sons of light and sons of the day..." The Grace.

THE SECOND LETTER OF PAUL TO THE THESSALONIANS

|1| Salutation. "We are bound to give thanks to God always for you, brethren..."
|2| "Stand firm and hold to the traditions which you were taught by us..."
|3| "Keep away from any brother who is living in idleness..." The Grace.

THE FIRST LETTER OF PAUL TO TIMOTHY

|1| Salutation. "Christ Jesus came into the world to save sinners..."
|2| "In every place men should pray, lifting holy hands without anger..."
|3| The office of a bishop. The office of a deacon.
|4| "Let no one despise your youth..." "Do not neglect the gift you have..."
|5| Concerning widows and elders.
|6| Concerning slaves. "We brought nothing into this world..." The Grace.

THE SECOND LETTER OF PAUL TO TIMOTHY

|1| Salutation. "Follow the pattern of sound words which you have heard from me..."
|2| "You then, my son, be strong in the grace that is in Christ Jesus..."
|3| "In the last days there will come times of stress."
|4| "I have fought the good fight, I have finished the race, I have kept the faith."

THE LETTER OF PAUL TO TITUS

1. Salutation. "This is why I left you in Crete, that you might amend..."
2. "Declare these things; exhort and reprove with all authority. Let no one disregard you.
3. "I desire you to insist on these things..." Greetings. The Grace.

THE LETTER OF PAUL TO PHILEMON

☐ Salutation. "I appeal to you for my child, Onesimus..." Greetings. The Grace.

THE LETTER TO THE HEBREWS

1. "God spoke of old to our fathers by the prophets; but in these last days..."
2. "Therefore we must pay closer attention to what we have heard..."
3. "Consider Jesus, the apostle and high priest of our confession..."
4. "Let us therefore strive to enter that rest..."
5. "...being designated by God a high priest after the order of Melchizedek."
6. "Therefore let us leave the elementary doctrines of Christ and go on to maturity..."
7. "For this Melchizedek, king of Salem, priest of the most high God, met Abraham..."
8. "We have such a high priest, one who is seated at the right hand..."
9. "But when Christ appeared...he entered once for all into the Holy Place..."
10. "When Christ had offered for all time a single sacrifice for sins..."
11. "Now faith is the assurance of things hoped for, the conviction of things not seen."
12. "Therefore, since we are surrounded by so great a cloud of witnesses..."
13. "Now may the God of peace who brought again from the dead..." Greetings. The Grace.

THE LETTER OF JAMES

1. Salutation. "If any one thinks he is religious, and does not bridle his tongue..."
2. "For as the body apart from the spirit is dead, so faith apart from works is dead."
3. "So the tongue is a little member and boasts of great things."
4. "You ought to say, 'If the Lord wills, we shall live and we shall do this or that.'"
5. "Be patient, therefore, brethren, until the coming of the Lord."

THE FIRST LETTER OF PETER

1 Salutation. "You have been born anew, not of perishable seed but of imperishable..."
2 "You are a chosen race, a royal priesthood, a holy nation, God's own people..."
3 "For it is better to suffer for doing right...than for doing wrong..."
4 "Beloved, do not be surprised at the fiery ordeal which comes upon you..."
5 "Humble yourselves therefore under the mighty hand of God..." Greetings. Peace.

THE SECOND LETTER OF PETER

1 Salutation. "For we did not follow cleverly devised myths..."
2 "But false prophets also arose among the people..."
3 "This is now the second letter that I have written to you, beloved..."

THE FIRST LETTER OF JOHN

1 "That which was from the beginning, which we have heard, which we have seen..."
2 "My little children, I am writing this to you so that you may not sin..."
3 "This is the message which you have heard...that we should love one another..."
4 "We love, because he first loved us."
5 "Every one who believes that Jesus is the Christ is a child of God..."

THE SECOND LETTER OF JOHN

☐ "The elder to the elect lady and her children, whom I love in truth..."

THE THIRD LETTER OF JOHN

☐ "The elder to the beloved Gaius, whom I love in the truth..."

THE LETTER OF JUDE

☐ Salutation. "In the last time there will be scoffers..." Ascription.

1	Preface. "John to the seven churches that are in Asia..."
2	Letters to Ephesus, Smyrna, Pergamum, Thyatira.
3	Letters to Sardis, Philadelphia, Laodicea.
4	Vision of the heavenly worship of God.
5	Vision of the heavenly worship of the Lamb.
6	Seven seals: White, red, black, pale horses, martyrs' lament, cosmic disasters.
7	Sealing of servants of God. The great multitude of martyrs.
8	Seven angels with seven trumpets. Hail, fire; burning mountain; falling star; darkness;
9	Locusts; horsemen from Euphrates.
10	John eats the scroll given to him by the angel.
11	The two witnesses. The seventh trumpet.
12	"A woman clothed with the sun, with the moon under her feet..." Michael and dragon.
13	Beast from the sea. Beast from the earth.
14	Seven visions.
15	Seven angels and seven plagues.
16	Seven bowls of the wrath of God.
17	Judgment of the great harlot.
18	Fall of Babylon is proclaimed.
19	Hymns of praise. Vision of the Word of God. Beast is captured.
20	Satan bound. Last Judgment. Gog and Magog.
21	New heaven and a new earth. New Jerusalem.
22	River of the water of life. "Surely I am coming soon."

II.
THE HISTORICAL TIME-LINE OF THE BIBLICAL PERIOD

II. THE HISTORICAL TIME-LINE OF THE BIBLICAL PERIOD

A. TWO THOUSAND YEARS AT A GLANCE

The history of the biblical period may be pictured as a time-line
which begins almost two thousand years before the birth of Christ (see
Fig. No.1). Although it is difficult to be precise about the Patriarchal
Period, most scholars would say that it is probable that Abraham, Isaac
and Jacob should be placed in Palestine somewhere around the 19th or the
18th centuries B.C. Their descendants, the Hebrews later to become known
as the Israelites, immigrate into Egypt because of a severe famine.
After a sojourn there that lasts for approximately four centuries, the Hebrews
become slaves of the Egyptians. They are led out of this bondage by
Moses in the Exodus. They wander in the Wilderness of Sinai until they
come to the land of Canaan. Because they believe this land to have
been promised to them by God, they conquer it so that it may become
their permanent home. The period of the Conquest is followed by a
period in which Israel is ruled by a series of "judges." By the
11th century B.C. the need for the unification of the state becomes
evident in the face of the threat from Israel's enemies, the Philistines,
and, as a consequence, Saul is made the first king. Saul is succeeded
by David, who establishes a royal dynasty, the "House of David." He is
succeeded by his son, Solomon, who builds the first Temple. After the
death of Solomon the kingdom divides into two states, Israel in the
north and Judah in the south. By the end of the 8th century B.C. the
northern kingdom has been carried away by the conquering Assyrians and
Judah is left in the south. However, Judah itself is carried off in
Exile in the 6th century B.C. by the Babylonians. In contrast to the

fate of Israel, Judah is allowed to return home during that same century. Judah remains under Persian domination until the 4th century B.C. when Alexander the Great begins the conquests which were to create the largest empire history had seen to this date. At the beginning of the 3rd century B.C. Palestine is governed by Ptolemaic rulers with their center of power in Egypt, and at the beginning of the 2nd century B.C., it is governed by the Seleucids with their center of power in Syria. However, in the first part of the 2nd century B.C. the Jews revolt against their rulers when they are ordered to give up their religious observances. This revolt under the leadership of Judas Maccabeus ushers in a period of independence which lasts until the land is conquered by the Romans around the middle of the 1st century B.C. The Romans remain the ruling power throughout the period of the New Testament during the 1st and 2nd centuries A.D.

Thus, in one glance we are able to make out the general shape of two thousand years of history. But if that history is to be of any use to us, we will have to examine it in more detail and from a closer point of observation.

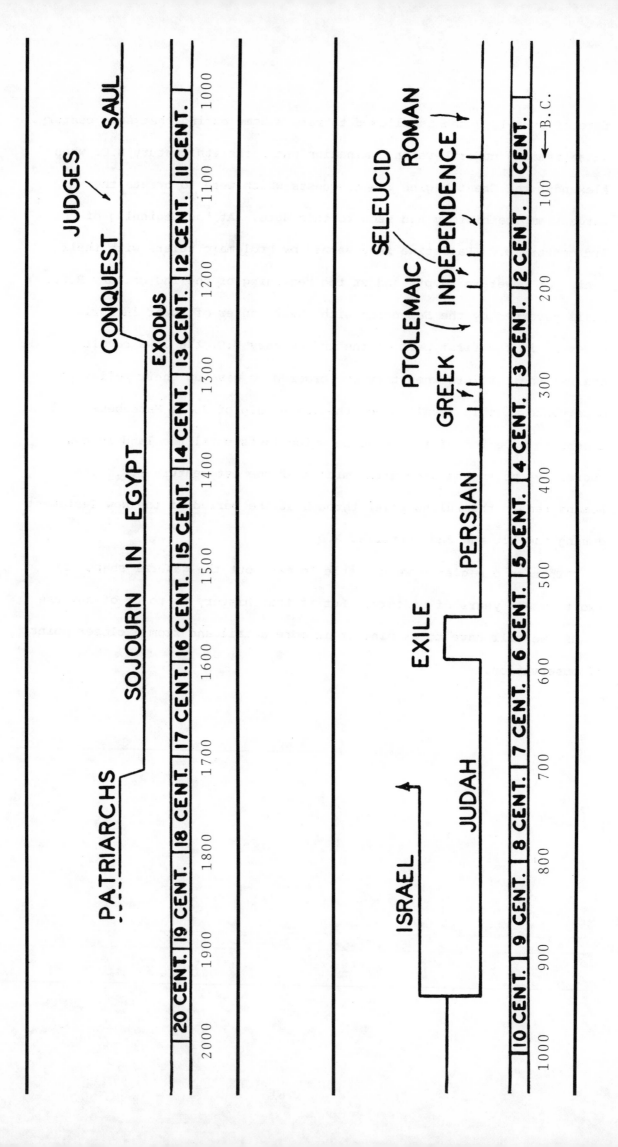

Fig. No.1

B. BIBLICAL HISTORY--A CENTURY TO A PAGE

A closer look at the historical events related to the biblical story may be had by changing the scale of the time-line. The following time-line has each century represented by a page, and each 10 years represented by one inch. The center line indicates the succession of rulers, the major characters and the main events that are associated with the people of Israel and the early Christian Church. The uppermost line represents the events and characters that have to do with the ruling powers in the areas generally to the north (Mesopotamia, Asia Minor, Syria and in the later centuries Rome). The lower line represents characters and events which took place in the south in Egypt. Occasionally contemporary archaeological artifacts which illuminate particular centuries are indicated on the pages that deal with those centuries. The books of the Old Testament are represented as gray scrolls; the books of the Apocrypha are represented as white scrolls; and the books of the New Testament are represented as smaller gray scrolls.

The purpose of this time-line is not to relate a history of the people of the Bible. That is better done by a conventional text written with that specific intention. The purpose of the time-line is to provide a means of visualizing the events connected with that history, and it is better used in conjunction with a good history of the biblical period.

The results of a critical approach to the Bible have been assumed throughout the preparation of this time-line. The dates of the composition of the various books of the Bible must not be considered to be as precise as their location on the page above a specific year might seem to indicate, and, consequently, a good introduction to the Bible should be consulted for more detailed information.

ASSYRIA HAS COLONIES IN CAPPADOCIA

CAPPADOCIAN TEXTS (19th cent. BC)
Thousands of tablets found at Kanish (Kültpe) which indicate that Assyrians were trading in Asia Minor in this period. The word "Khapiru" appears in these texts.

TEXTS OF 1st DYNASTY OF BABYLON
(from 19th to 16th cent. BC)
Many thousands of tablets which illustrate history of Babylon.

LAW CODE OF
LIPIT ISHTAR

ESHNUNNA
LAW CODE

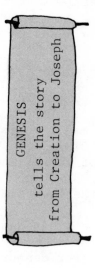

ISAAC

date approximate

ABRAHAM   (in Palestine)

date approximate

PRIMEVAL PERIOD

THE PATRIARCHS

GENESIS
tells the story
from Creation to Joseph

MIDDLE KINGDOM   (XII DYNASTY, ca. 1991-1786)   Period of prosperity and stability; Egyptian control extends over Palestine

19TH CENTURY B.C.

| 1900 | 1890 | 1880 | 1870 | 1860 | 1850 | 1840 | 1830 | 1820 | 1810 | 1800 |

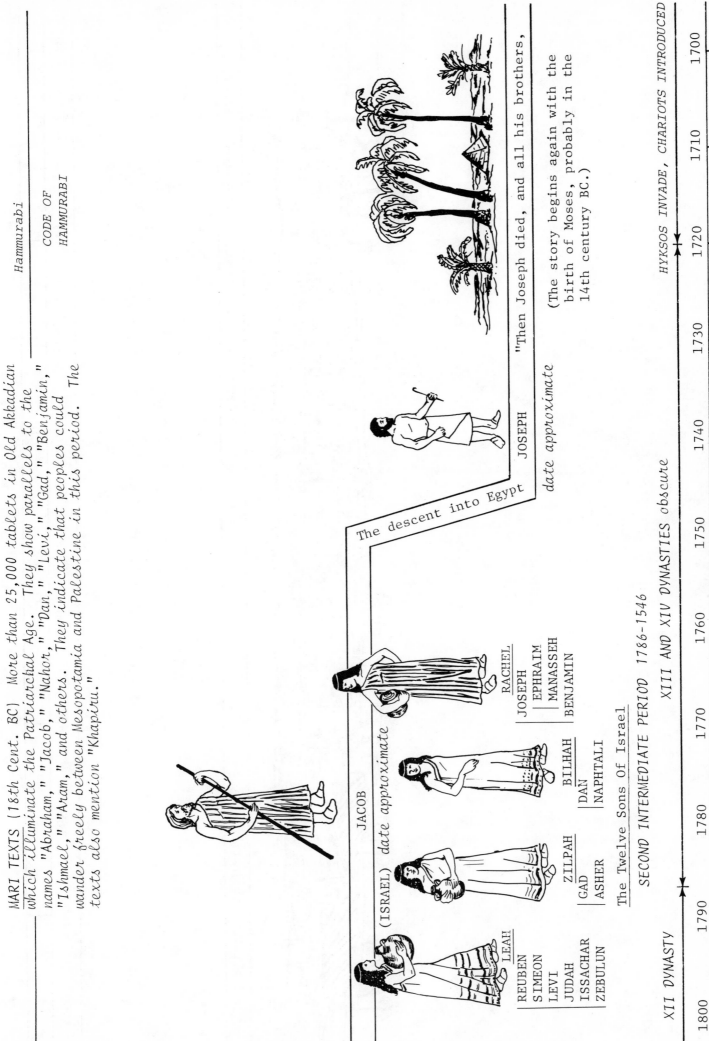

MARI TEXTS (18th Cent. BC) More than 25,000 tablets in Old Akkadian which illuminate the Patriarchal Age. They show parallels to the names "Abraham," "Jacob," "Nahor," "Dan," "Levi," "Gad," "Benjamin," "Ishmael," "Aram," and others. They indicate that peoples could wander freely between Mesopotamia and Palestine in this period. The texts also mention "Khapiru."

Hammurabi

CODE OF HAMMURABI

"Then Joseph died, and all his brothers,

(The story begins again with the birth of Moses, probably in the 14th century BC.)

JOSEPH

The descent into Egypt

date approximate

JACOB

(ISRAEL) date approximate

LEAH
REUBEN
SIMEON
LEVI
JUDAH
ISSACHAR
ZEBULUN

ZILPAH
GAD
ASHER

BILHAH
DAN
NAPHTALI

RACHEL
JOSEPH
EPHRAIM
MANASSEH
BENJAMIN

The Twelve Sons Of Israel

SECOND INTERMEDIATE PERIOD 1786-1546

XIII AND XIV DYNASTIES obscure

HYKSOS INVADE, CHARIOTS INTRODUCED

XII DYNASTY

1800   1790   1780   1770   1760   1750   1740   1730   1720   1710   1700

18TH CENTURY B.C.

ALALAKH TABLETS (17th Cent. BC) Several thousand
texts which mention that the "Khapiru" are in
Upper Mesopotamia during the Patriarchal Age

OLD BABYLONIAN EMPIRE

But the descendants of Israel were fruitful and increased greatly;

and all that generation

HYKSOS RULE IN EGYPT

XV DYNASTY

| 1700 | 1690 | 1680 | 1670 | 1660 | 1650 | 1640 | 1630 | 1620 | 1610 | 1600 |

17TH CENTURY B.C.

FIRST AMORITE DYNASTY IN BABYLON

they multiplied and grew exceedingly strong;

NEW KINGDOM (XVIII DYNASTY ca. 1570-1310)

Hyksos expelled

Thutmosis I built first tomb in Valley of the Kings

Amenophis I

Amosis

| 1600 | 1590 | 1580 | 1570 | 1560 | 1550 | 1540 | 1530 | 1520 | 1510 | 1500 |

16TH CENTURY B.C.

CASSITE DYNASTY IN BABYLON

NUZI TABLETS (15th Cent. BC) Several thousand
texts which show that Assyrian kings ruled all
of Upper Mesopotamia in this period. They also
mention the "Khapiru."

so that the land was filled with them.

EGYPT'S GOLDEN AGE

Campaigns in Syria; conquers Megiddo, Joppa; erects four
stelae (called Cleopatra's Needles today)

Thutmosis III   Amenophis II   Thutmosis IV

1500   1490   1480   1470   1460   1450   1440   1430   1420   1410   1400

15TH CENTURY B.C.

AMARNA LETTERS (14th Cent. BC) Tablets describing the "Khapiru" as "disturbers of the peace."

BOGHAZKÖY TEXTS (14th Cent. BC) Tablets in Hittite which mention "Khapiru."

RAS SHAMRA TEXTS (15-13th Cent. BC) Tablets in the Canaanite language written in an alphabet composed of cuneiform characters. They contain the myths and epics of Canaan. They also mention the "Khapiru."

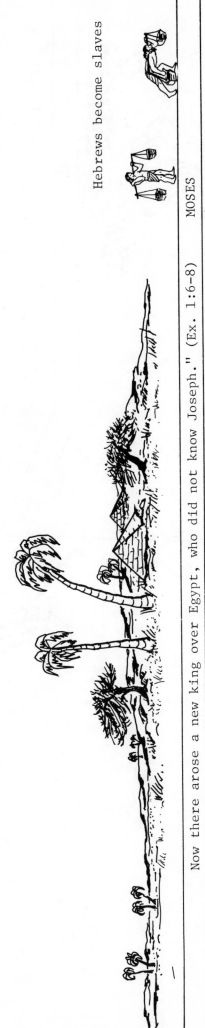

Hebrews become slaves

MOSES

Hidden in a basket made of bulrushes

"Now there arose a new king over Egypt, who did not know Joseph." (Ex. 1:6-8)

Religious reform (Aton worship); cuneiform tablets at Tell el-Amarna, the capital of the kingdom

A M A R N A   P E R I O D

Amenophis III		Amenophis IV (Akhenaten)	Toutankhamon	Haremhab	XIX DYN 1310-1200 Sethos I	
1400	1390	1380	1370	1360	1350	1340	1330	1320	1310	1300

14TH CENTURY B.C.

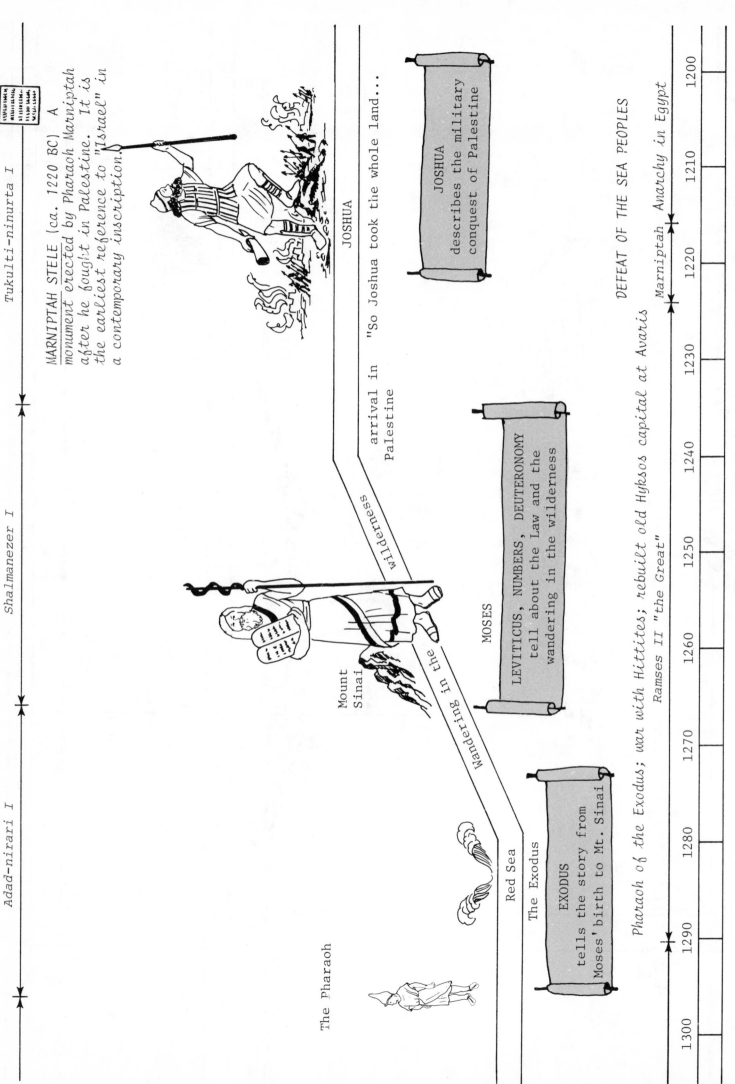

Adad-nirari I   Shalmanezer I   Tukulti-ninurta I

MARNIPTAH STELE (ca. 1220 BC) A monument erected by Pharaoh Marniptah after he fought in Palestine. It is the earliest reference to "Israel" in a contemporary inscription.

The Pharaoh

Red Sea

The Exodus

EXODUS
tells the story from Moses' birth to Mt. Sinai

Mount Sinai

Wandering in the wilderness

MOSES

LEVITICUS, NUMBERS, DEUTERONOMY tell about the Law and the wandering in the wilderness

arrival in Palestine

JOSHUA

"So Joshua took the whole land..."

JOSHUA
describes the military conquest of Palestine

Pharaoh of the Exodus; war with Hittites; rebuilt old Hyksos capital at Avaris
Ramses II "the Great"

Marniptah Anarchy in Egypt

DEFEAT OF THE SEA PEOPLES

1300   1290   1280   1270   1260   1250   1240   1230   1220   1210   1200

13TH CENTURY B.C.

A S S Y R I A N   W E A K N E S S

OTHNIEL   EHUD   (Shamgar)   DEBORAH   GIDEON (Tola) (Jair)

"...and the land had rest from war."
(Joshua 11:23)

"In those days there was no king in Israel..."

JUDGES
describes the rules of
the judges

(Between 1200 and 900 B.C. there is an eclipse of the great empires of the Near East.)

A second invasion of Sea Peoples; they
are defeated by Ramesses III

Philistines settle in Palestine

XX DYNASTY 1180-1065

Ramesses III   Ramesses IV-XI (to 1065)

1200	1190	1180	1170	1160	1150	1140	1130	1120	1110	1100

12TH CENTURY B.C.

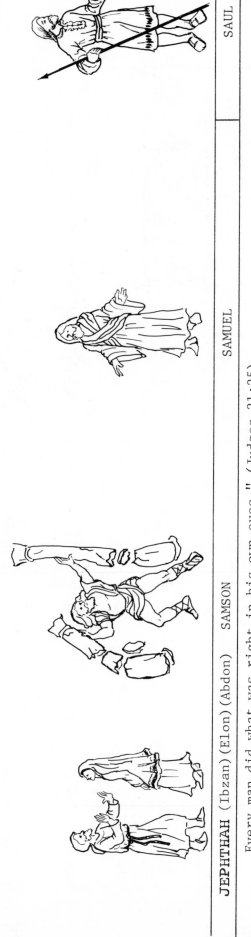

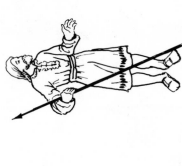

JEPHTHAH (Ibzan) (Elon) (Abdon)   SAMSON   SAMUEL   SAUL

Every man did what was right in his own eyes." (Judges 21:25)

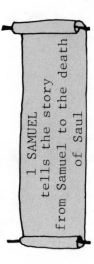

1 SAMUEL
tells the story
from Samuel to the death
of Saul

XXI DYNASTY 1065-935

1100	1090	1080	1070	1060	1050	1040	1030	1020	1010	1000

11TH CENTURY B.C.

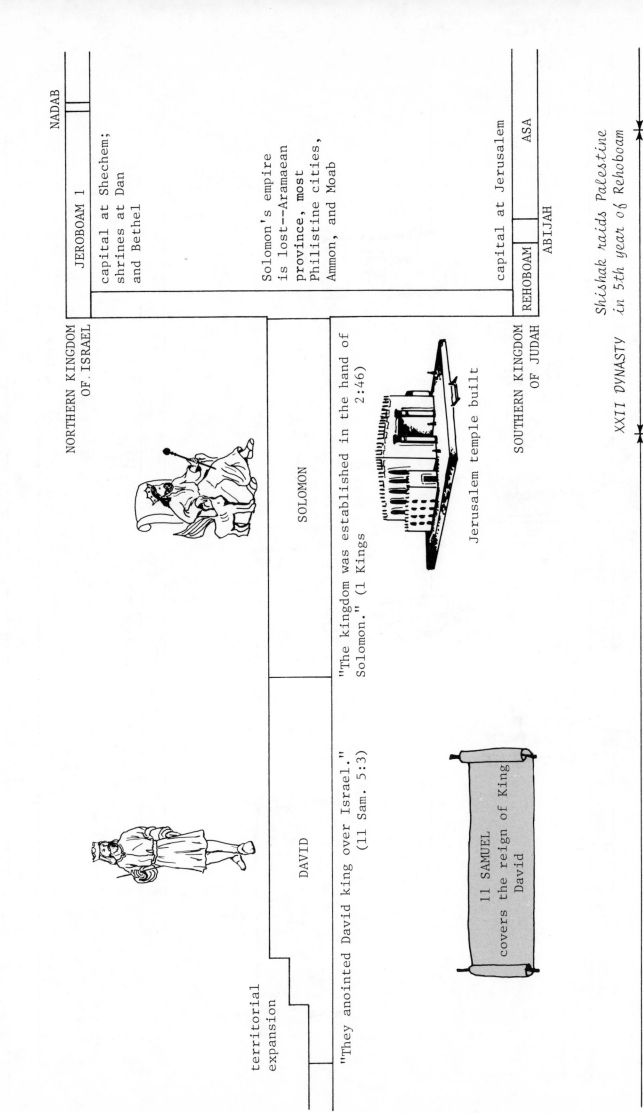

PERIOD OF ASSYRIAN WEAKNESS

BEGINNING OF ASSYRIAN RECOVERY

Asshur-dan II *Adad-nirari II*

NADAB

JEROBOAM 1

capital at Shechem;
shrines at Dan
and Bethel

NORTHERN KINGDOM
OF ISRAEL

Solomon's empire
is lost--Aramaean
province, most
Philistine cities,
Ammon, and Moab

territorial
expansion

DAVID

SOLOMON

"They anointed David king over Israel."
(11 Sam. 5:3)

"The kingdom was established in the hand of
Solomon." (1 Kings
2:46)

Jerusalem temple built

11 SAMUEL
covers the reign of King
David

capital at Jerusalem

REHOBOAM

ABIJAH

ASA

SOUTHERN KINGDOM
OF JUDAH

*Shishak raids Palestine
in 5th year of Rehoboam*

XXII DYNASTY

1000   990   980   970   960   950   940   930   920   910   900

10TH CENTURY B.C.

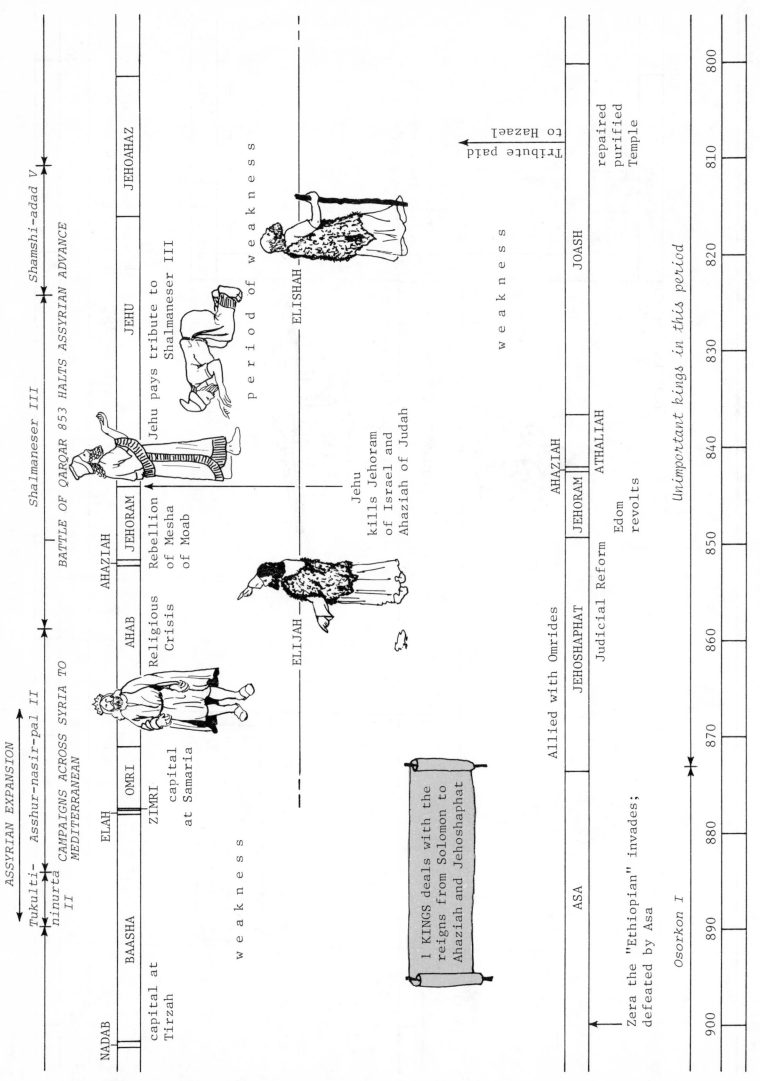

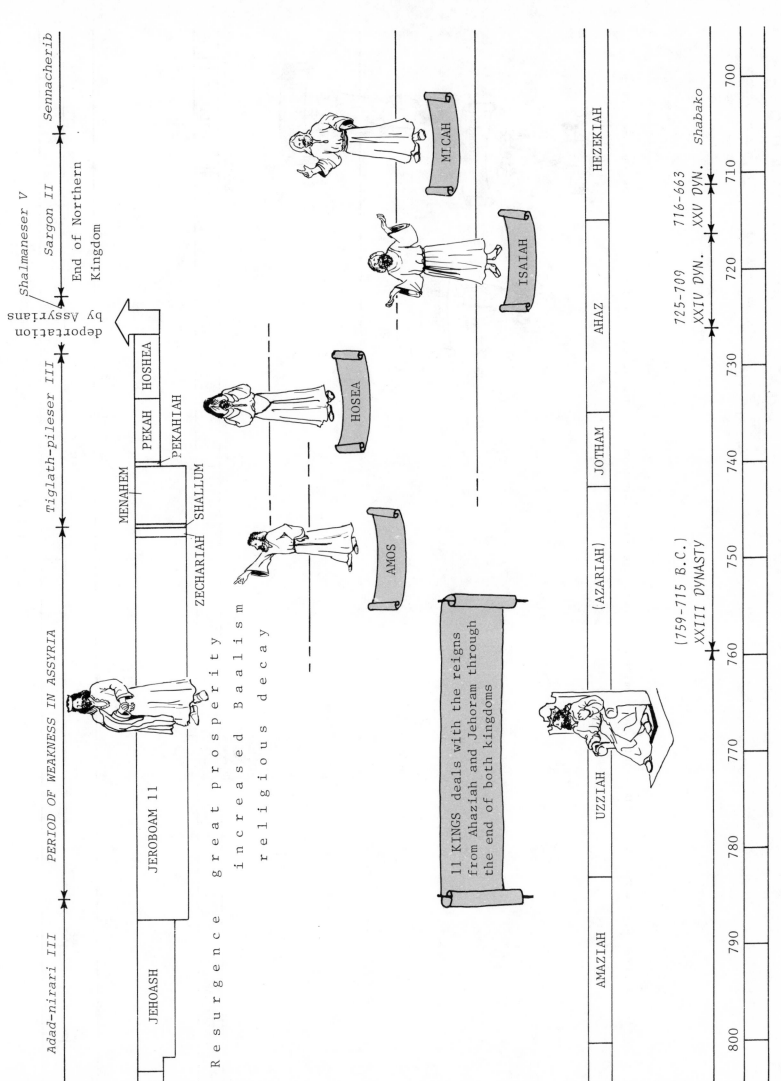

8TH CENTURY B.C.

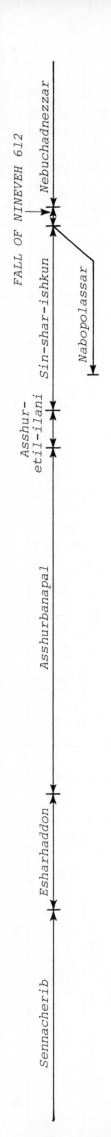
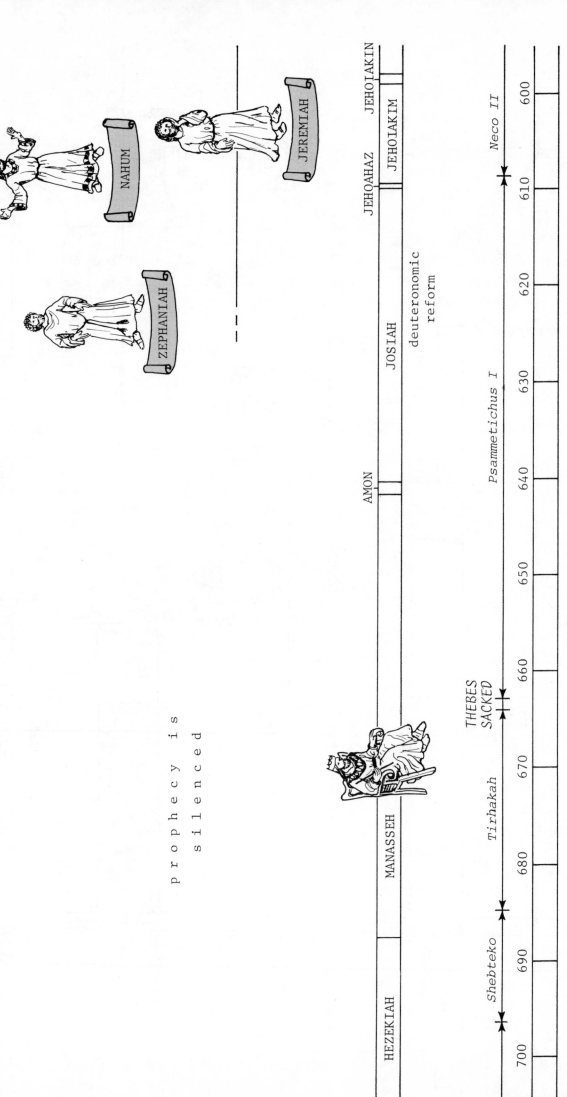

FALL OF NINEVEH 612

Sennacherib Esharhaddon Asshurbanapal Asshur-etil-ilani Sin-shar-ishkun Nebuchadnezzar

Nabopolassar

The Israelites who remained in the north were mixed with people from Babylonia, Hamath, etc. and eventually become Samaritans

NAHUM

ZEPHANIAH

JEREMIAH

prophecy is silenced

HEZEKIAH MANASSEH AMON JOSIAH JEHOAHAZ JEHOIAKIM JEHOIAKIN

deuteronomic reform

Shebteko Tirhakah Psammetichus I Neco II

THEBES SACKED

700 690 680 670 660 650 640 630 620 610 600

7TH CENTURY B.C.

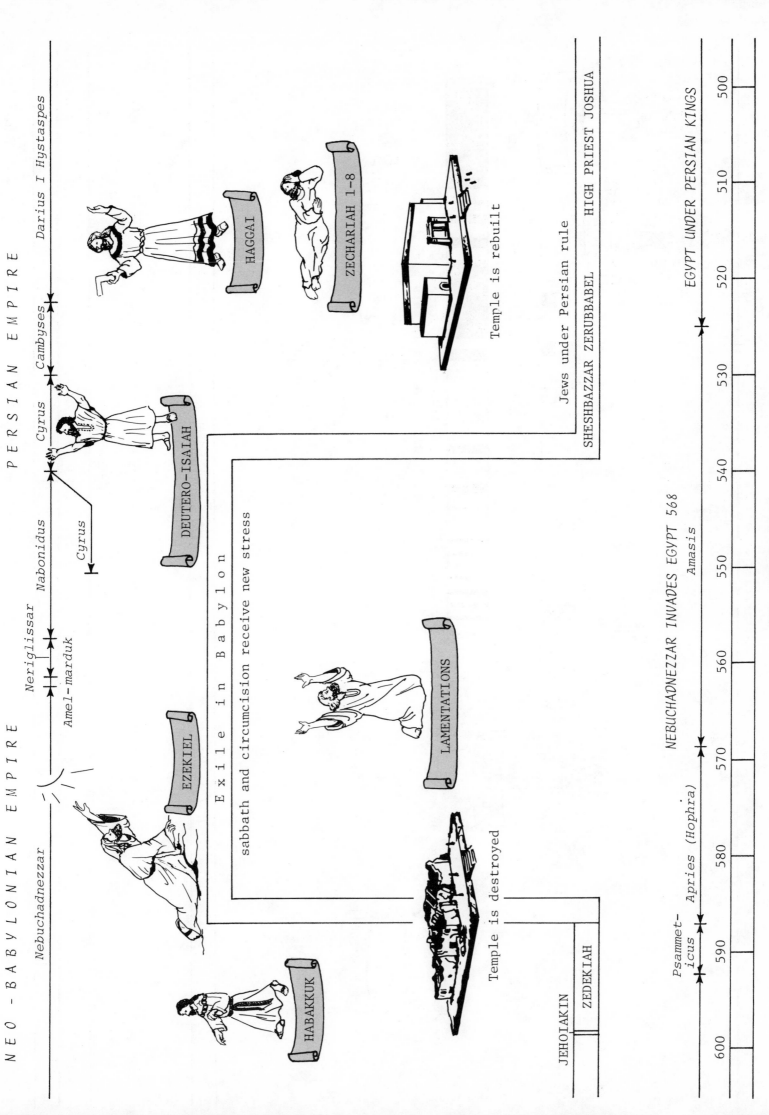

NEO-BABYLONIAN EMPIRE

PERSIAN EMPIRE

Nebuchadnezzar • Neriglissar • Nabonidus • Cyrus • Cambyses • Darius I Hystaspes
Amel-marduk

Cyrus

HABAKKUK

EZEKIEL

DEUTERO-ISAIAH

HAGGAI

ZECHARIAH 1-8

Exile in Babylon

sabbath and circumcision receive new stress

LAMENTATIONS

Temple is destroyed

Temple is rebuilt

JEHOIAKIN
ZEDEKIAH

SHESHBAZZAR ZERUBBABEL   HIGH PRIEST JOSHUA

Jews under Persian rule

NEBUCHADNEZZAR INVADES EGYPT 568

EGYPT UNDER PERSIAN KINGS

Psammet-icus Apries (Hophra) Amasis

600   590   580   570   560   550   540   530   520   510   500

6TH CENTURY B.C.

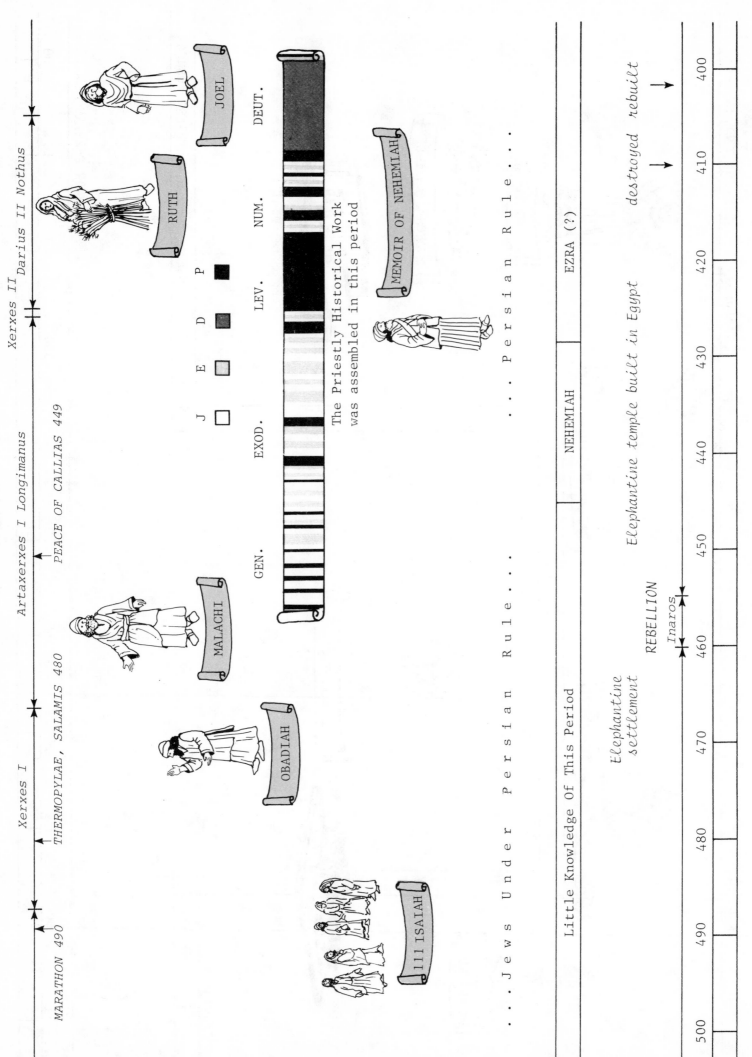

MARATHON 490

Xerxes I

THERMOPYLAE, SALAMIS 480

Artaxerxes I Longimanus

PEACE OF CALLIAS 449

Xerxes II Darius II Nothus

III ISAIAH

OBADIAH

MALACHI

RUTH

JOEL

J E D P

GEN. EXOD. LEV. NUM. DEUT.

The Priestly Historical Work
was assembled in this period

MEMOIR OF NEHEMIAH

. . . J e w s   U n d e r   P e r s i a n   R u l e . . . . P e r s i a n   R u l e . . . .

Little Knowledge Of This Period

NEHEMIAH   EZRA (?)

Elephantine
settlement

REBELLION
Inaros

Elephantine temple built in Egypt

destroyed   rebuilt

500   490   480   470   460   450   440   430   420   410   400

5TH CENTURY B.C.

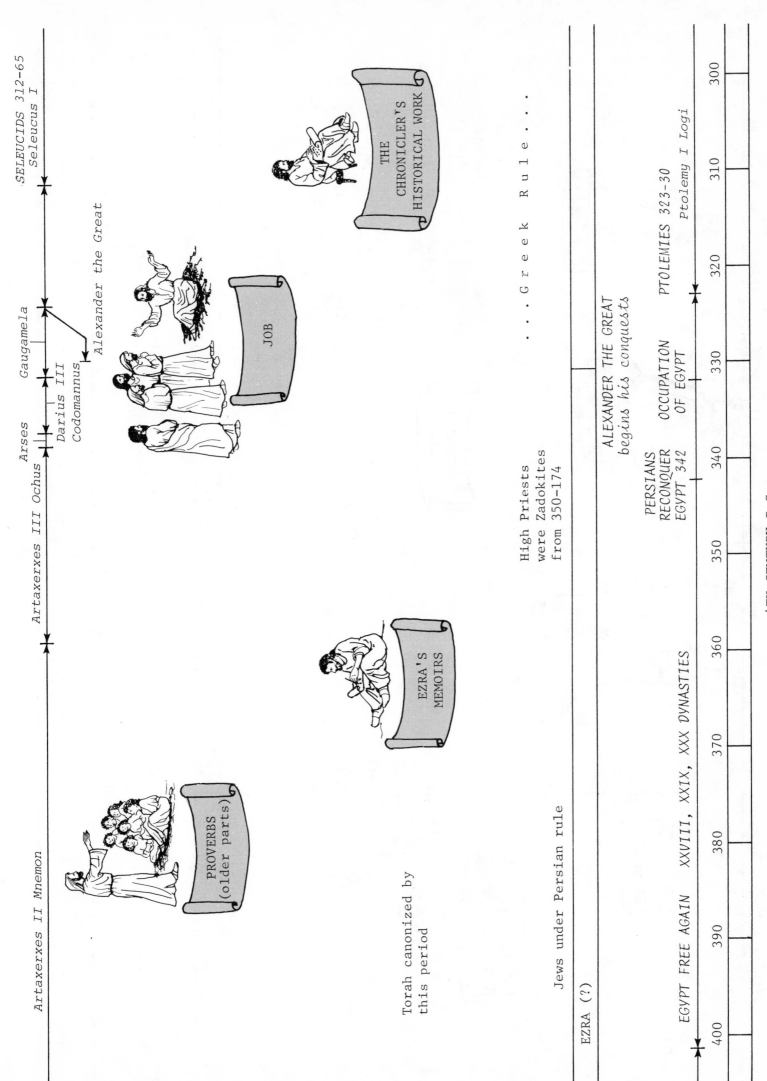

SELEUCIDS 312-65
Seleucus I

Artaxerxes III Ochus

Artaxerxes II Mnemon

Arses

Gaugamela

Darius III
Codomannus

Alexander the Great

THE
CHRONICLER'S
HISTORICAL WORK

JOB

EZRA'S
MEMOIRS

PROVERBS
(older parts)

Torah canonized by
this period

High Priests
were Zadokites
from 350-174

Jews under Persian rule

EGYPT FREE AGAIN   XXVIII, XXIX, XXX DYNASTIES

PERSIANS
RECONQUER
EGYPT 342

OCCUPATION
OF EGYPT

PTOLEMIES 323-30
Ptolemy I Logi

ALEXANDER THE GREAT
begins his conquests

. . . G r e e k   R u l e . . . .

EZRA (?)

400   390   380   370   360   350   340   330   320   310   300

4TH CENTURY B.C.

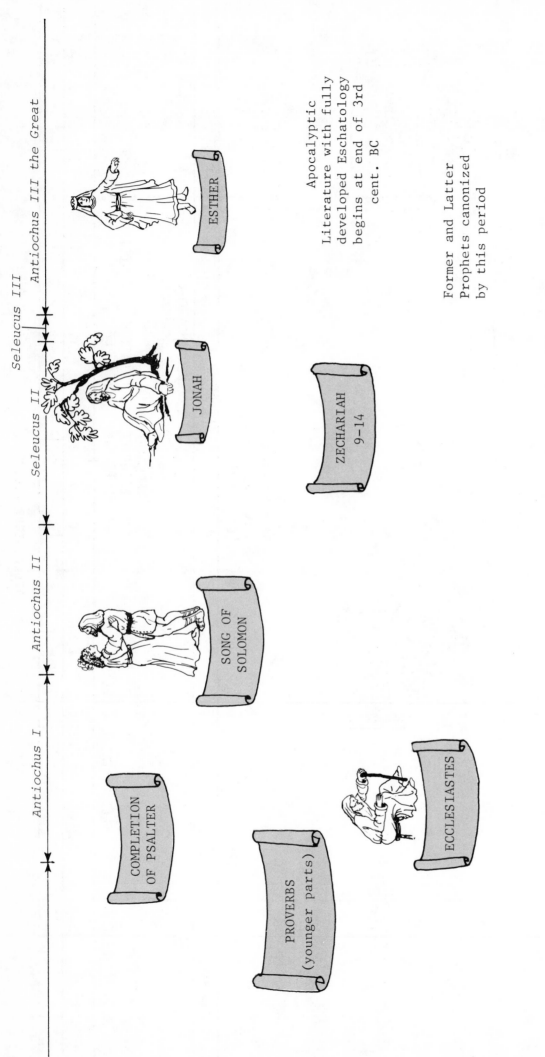

Antiochus III the Great

Seleucus III

Antiochus III the Great

ESTHER

Seleucus II

JONAH

ZECHARIAH
9-14

Apocalyptic
Literature with fully
developed Eschatology
begins at end of 3rd
cent. BC

Former and Latter
Prophets canonized
by this period

Antiochus II

SONG OF
SOLOMON

Antiochus I

COMPLETION
OF PSALTER

PROVERBS
(younger parts)

ECCLESIASTES

LXX translation of OT from Hebrew to Greek, 3rd cent.-132 BC

Palestine Under Ptolemaic Control

Ptolemy IV
Philopator

Ptolemy III Euergetes

Ptolemy II Philadelphus

200

210

220

230

240

250

260

270

280

290

300

3RD CENTURY B.C.

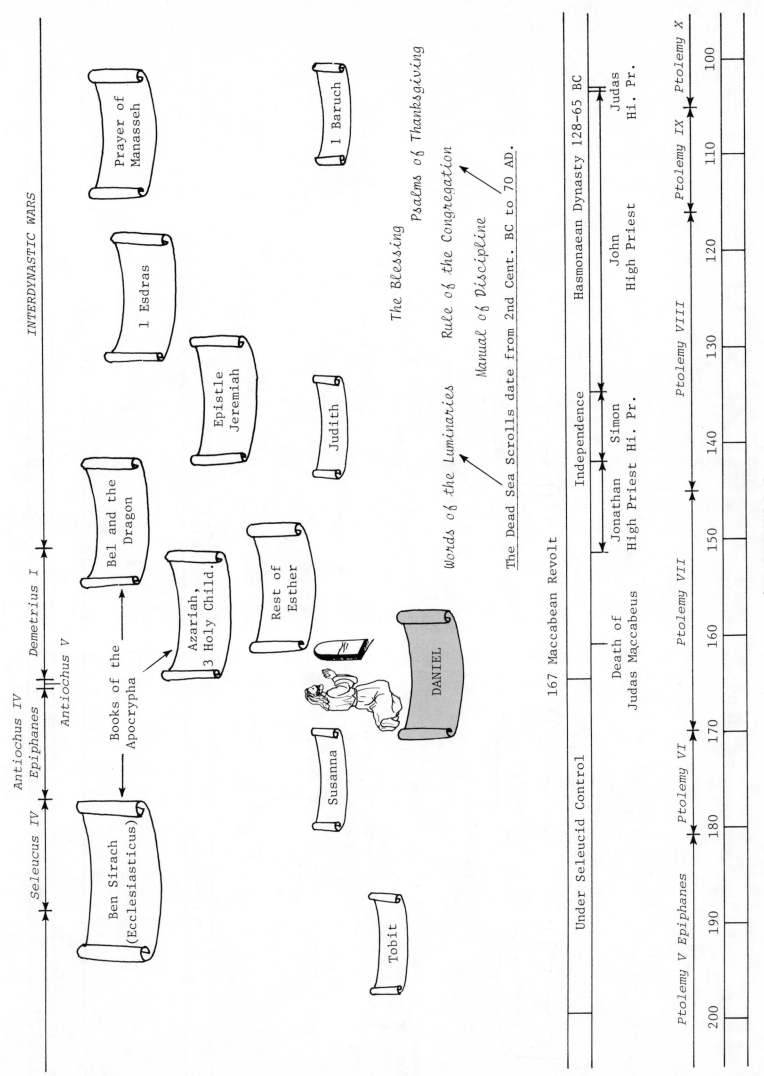

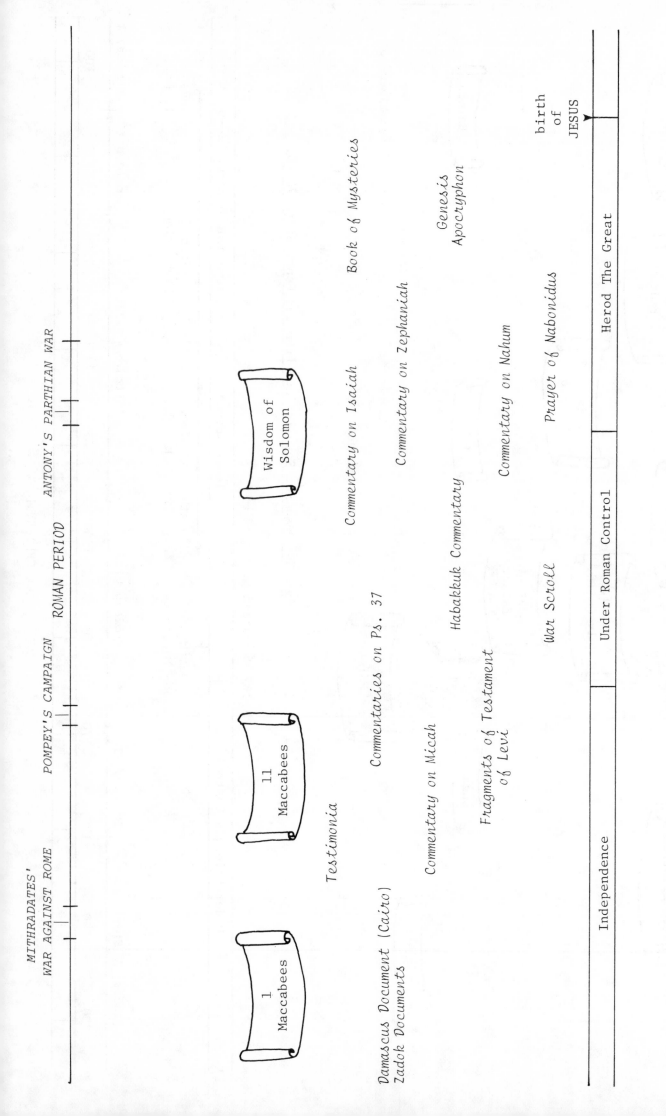

MITHRADATES'
WAR AGAINST ROME   POMPEY'S CAMPAIGN   ANTONY'S PARTHIAN WAR

ROMAN PERIOD

Wisdom of Solomon

Book of Mysteries

Commentary on Isaiah

Commentary on Zephaniah

Genesis Apocryphon

Commentary on Nahum

Commentary on Ps. 37

Prayer of Nabonidus

11 Maccabees

Habakkuk Commentary

Commentary on Micah

Fragments of Testament of Levi

War Scroll

Testimonia

*Damascus Document (Cairo)
Zadok Documents*

1 Maccabees

birth of JESUS

Herod The Great

Under Roman Control

Independence

EGYPT CONQUERED BY ROME

Cleopatra VII

Ptolemy XII

Ptolemy XI

0   10   20   30   40   50   60   70   80   90   100

1ST CENTURY B.C.

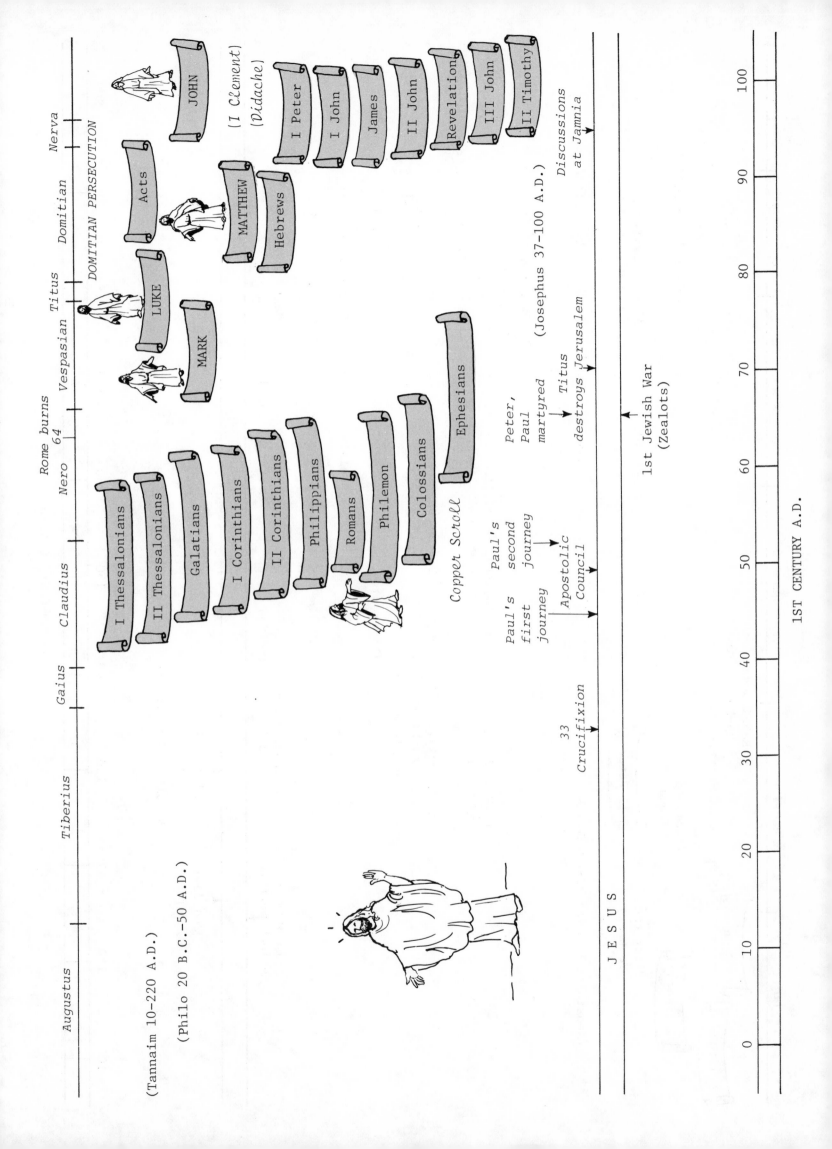

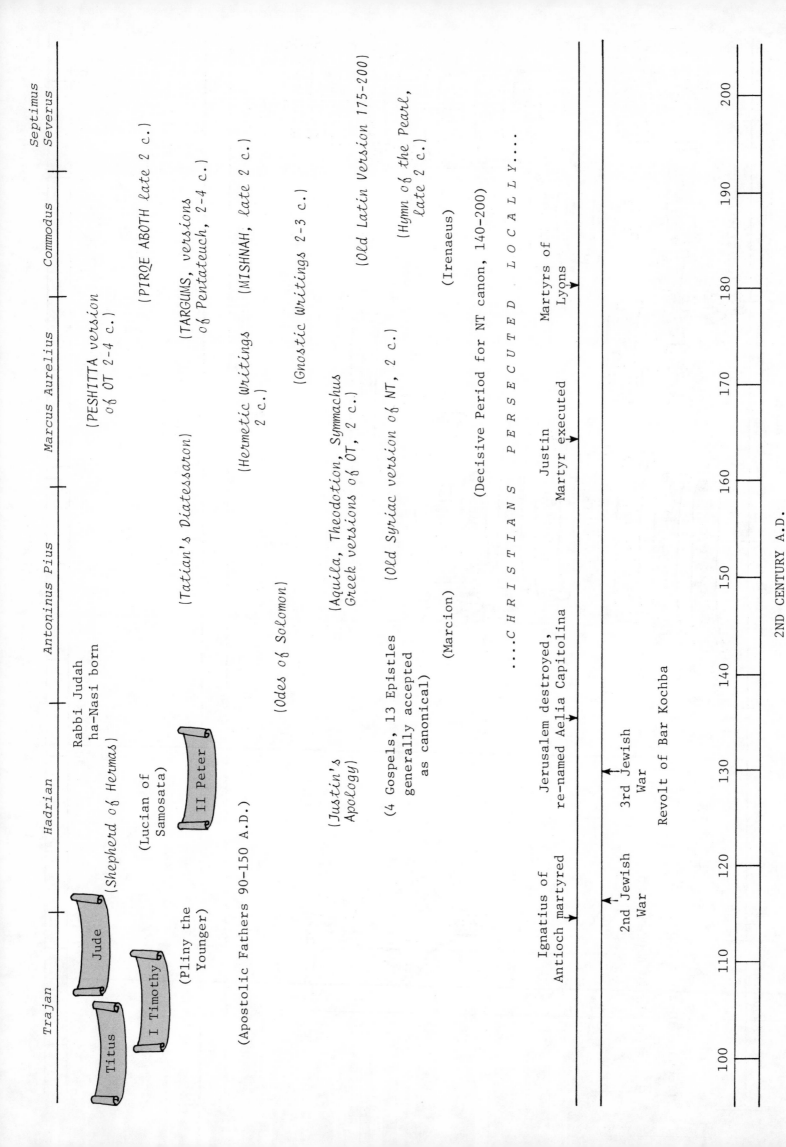

2ND CENTURY A.D.

III.
THE TOOLS OF BIBLICAL CRITICISM

III. THE TOOLS OF BIBLICAL CRITICISM

In Section I we have attempted to outline visually what is contained in the
books of the Bible. The primary emphasis in that section was the actual
content of the books. In Section II we have tried to see what the main
events and characters of the Bible would look like stretched out on a
time-line. The primary emphasis in that section was history. But in
Section III we will try to visualize what tools the biblical scholar
has at his disposal when he attempts to determine what the story means.
In other words, what are the tools of Biblical Criticism? It is not our
purpose to treat any of these disciplines exhaustively, but to arrange
them visually so that they may be seen as a whole and their interrelatedness
may become apparent.

At the outset Biblical Criticism can be divided into two main
divisions, Higher and Lower Criticism (see Fig No. 2). The terms "higher"
and "lower" imply no value judgment upon either division. One is not more
important than the other, nor is one more difficult than the other. The main
distinction between them is that Lower Criticism deals with the condition of
the written text itself (has the text been altered from its original state?),
whereas Higher Criticism deals with the more abstract problem of the meaning
of the text, seen in the light of literary and historical considerations.
Each of these levels of Biblical Criticism, both Higher and Lower, is dependent
upon the other. The scholars in one field must know something of the results
of the work of the scholars in the other field in order for their own
work to be fully informed.

The arrangement of the chart in Fig. No. 2 needs some explanation.
Most charts are arranged so that they may be read from the top to the
bottom. This chart, however, is arranged to be read from the more concrete
to the more abstract--thus from the bottom to the top. The roots of

THE TOOLS OF
BIBLICAL CRITICISM

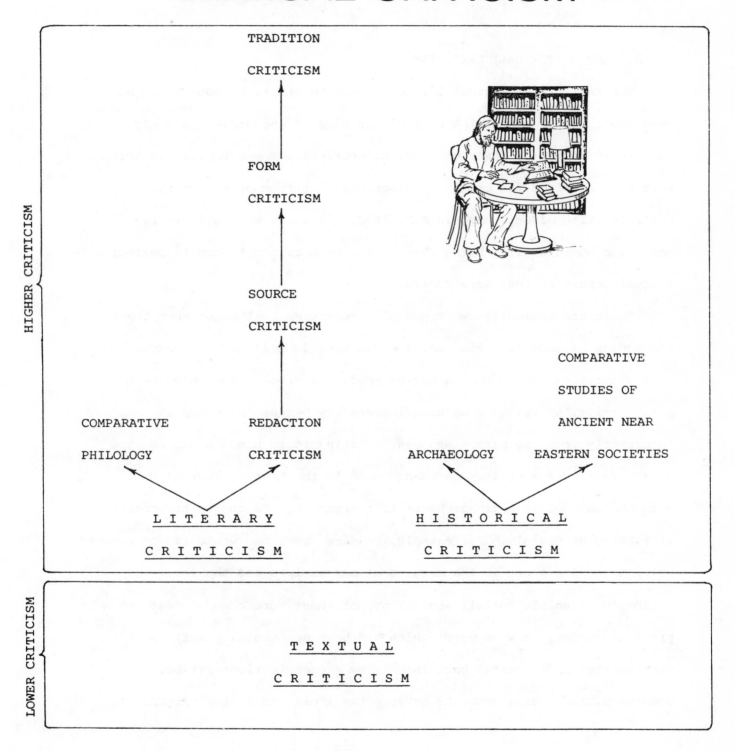

TRADITION

CRITICISM

HIGHER CRITICISM

FORM

CRITICISM

SOURCE

CRITICISM

COMPARATIVE   REDACTION   COMPARATIVE

PHILOLOGY   CRITICISM   STUDIES OF

ANCIENT NEAR

ARCHAEOLOGY   EASTERN SOCIETIES

L I T E R A R Y   H I S T O R I C A L

C R I T I C I S M   C R I T I C I S M

LOWER CRITICISM

T E X T U A L

C R I T I C I S M

Fig. No.2

the tree of Biblical Criticism are firmly planted in the concreteness

of the earth with Textual Criticism. However, the branches of Tradition

Criticism, for example, are very much in the abstract blue sky.

A. LOWER (TEXTUAL) CRITICISM

The task of the Textual Critic is made necessary because we do not

have the original manuscript of a single book of the Bible. We only

have later copies of these original manuscripts. These copies, in turn,

were not made from the original autographs, but from other copies.

Until the time of Gutenberg in A.D. 1450, all books were written by

hand, and human frailty being what it is, manuscripts tended to collect

textual errors as they were copied.

There are basically two types of alterations that occur when texts

are copied by hand (see Fig. No.3). One type is accidental in nature.

This alteration arises when a scribe reads incorrectly something from

a manuscript, or writes something incorrectly because he heard it

incorrectly from the person who was dictating it to him. A second type

of alteration is a deliberate change made in the text by someone who,

with the best of intentions, wants to correct it. He can either correct

it rightly or wrongly. For example, readers sometimes wrote random comments

between the lines and in the margins of manuscripts and the later

scribes were unable to tell whether or not these were comments made by a

previous reader, or were words which had been accidentally left out of

a manuscript and inserted back into it by a conscientious scribe.

Sometimes, therefore, comments between the lines and in the margins of

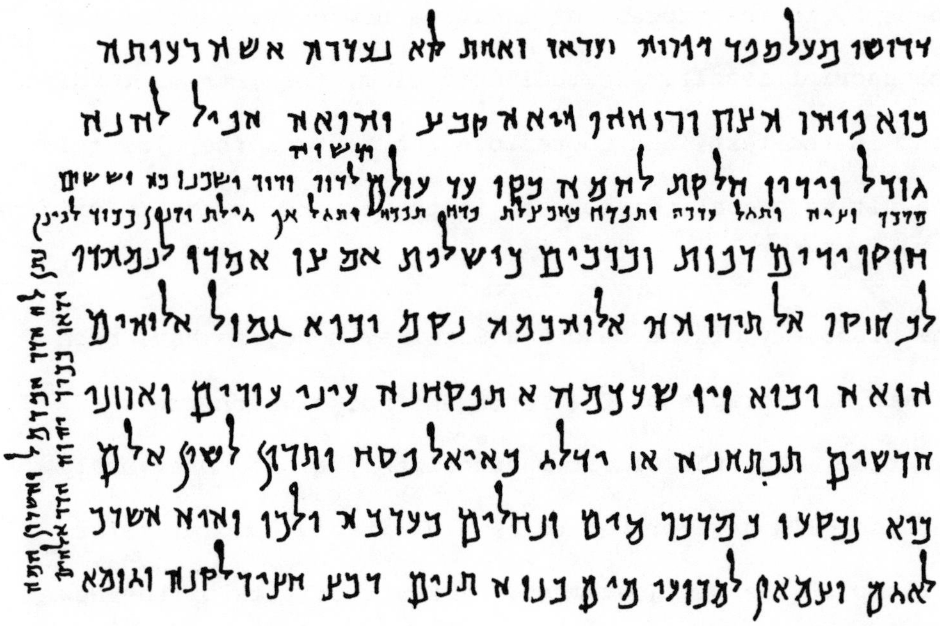

Textual Criticism tries to discover alterations in the
text and to restore the text to the oldest form possible.

TYPES OF ALTERATIONS

    1. Errors in copying arising from incorrect reading,
writing, or hearing by copyists.

    2. Deliberate changes made by copyists who wanted to
"correct" the text (either rightly or wrongly), or who
made comments in the margins which later copyists incorporated as
a part of the text itself.

TEXTUAL CRITICISM

Fig. No.3

manuscripts became, in the process of making a new copy, part of the text of the manuscript itself. Textual Criticism, then, tries to discover the alterations in the text, and to restore the text to the oldest form possible. The ultimate goal, of course, is to restore it to its original form.

Since the discovery of the Dead Sea Scrolls, scholars have been able to work with manuscripts of Old Testament books which are a thousand years older than the oldest manuscripts they had previously studied. These scrolls have proved to be a veritable gold mine for the Textual Critic of the Old Testament. Textual Critics of the New Testament, on the other hand, have always had a comparatively large number of manuscripts dating from an early period with which to work.

B. HIGHER CRITICISM

In contrast to Lower Criticism, Higher Criticism does not deal directly with the form of the written text but with the content of that text, and it deals with that content in historical and literary terms (see Fig. No.2).

Higher Criticism must be divided into the two categories of Literary and Historical Criticism because it is impossible to study the books themselves (Literary Criticism) without at the same time knowing something of the background against which these books were written (Historical Criticism). Therefore, Literary Criticism and Historical Criticism go hand in hand. We will discuss Historical Criticism first. It may be divided up into two disciplines, Archaeology and the Comparative Study of the Ancient Near East.

1. HISTORICAL CRITICISM

    a. ARCHAEOLOGY

The science of archaeology is employed to illuminate the content
of the text of the Bible by the physical evidence which may be obtained
from digging in the remains of the cultures which existed in the biblical
period. The primary purpose of archaeology is not to prove the Bible
"true," since theology is not "provable" by any science. On the
contrary, its main intention is to illuminate the Bible by revealing the
material remains associated with the daily life of biblical people and by
recovering data which can be used to fix the dates of the historical
events of the Bible. Archaeology has thrown a tremendous amount of
light upon the biblical scene in very concrete, tangible ways.

Originally archaeology was nothing more than a glorified
treasure hunt. Gradually, however, the methods of excavations, and
what is more important, the motives of excavations, greatly improved
throughout the years. Today the primary object of an excavation is not
to uncover beautiful things that will find their way into museums, but
to uncover tangible data about the way in which people lived in the biblical
period and about the kinds of historical events which left physical
evidence behind.

When a town was destroyed in ancient times by fire or earthquake,
or left abandoned for some reason, people would come back later to
rebuild on the same site. In this process they did not normally carry
away the ruins that were there. They merely smoothed them over and
built on top of them. As this process repeated itself over vast amounts
of time, town sites grew taller and taller and eventually became great
mounds, or "tells." When one slices into such a tell, one can see the

1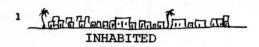
INHABITED

2
DESTROYED

3
DESERTED

4
INHABITED

5
DESTROYED

6
DESERTED

7
INHABITED

8
DESTROYED

9
DESERTED

10
INHABITED

11
DESTROYED

12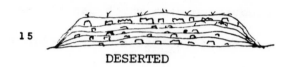
DESERTED

13
INHABITED

14
DESTROYED

15
DESERTED

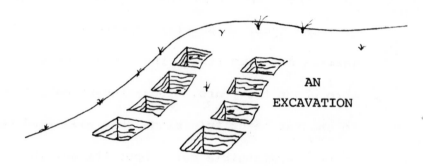

AN
EXCAVATION

Archaeology is a study of the material remains of the ancient world in order to throw light upon biblical history and culture.

ARCHAEOLOGY

Fig. No.4

layers left when the various cities were built one on top of the other (see Fig. No.4).

Archaeologists have discovered that the common potsherd, a broken piece of pottery, can serve as a valuable yardstick for the determining of the date of the layer in which it is found. Since pottery styles changed slowly over the centuries, a particular kind of pot may bear little resemblance in style to a similar pot made in a later century. Consequently, the lowly potsherd can be used to determine when that lay was originally a "walking surface," open to the sky. All that is below that layer was laid down earlier. All that is above that layer was laid down later. The artifacts found on that surface were laid down when that layer was a contemporary "now" to the people who lived in that period.

As we can see in Fig. No.5 the time-span covered by the Bible can be divided up into archaeological periods. The names for each period and the precise limits of those periods undergo shifts from time to time as more data are uncovered and evaluated by the archaeologists. However, the larger divisions have remained fairly constant. For a long time ancient man was compelled to use bronze as his primary metal for implements. Archaeologists have divided up this very long span of time into the Early (3000-2100 B.C.), Middle (2100-1550 B.C.) and Late (1550-1200 B.C.) Bronze Ages. Most scholars would date the Patriarchs, for instance, in the Middle Bronze Age ("Middle Bronze II A" in more precise archaeological terms). The Conquest of Canaan under Joshua took place during the Late Bronze Age. The Period of the Judges occurred during the beginning of the Iron Age (sometimes called the Israelite Period). At that time

ARCHAEOLOGICAL PERIODS

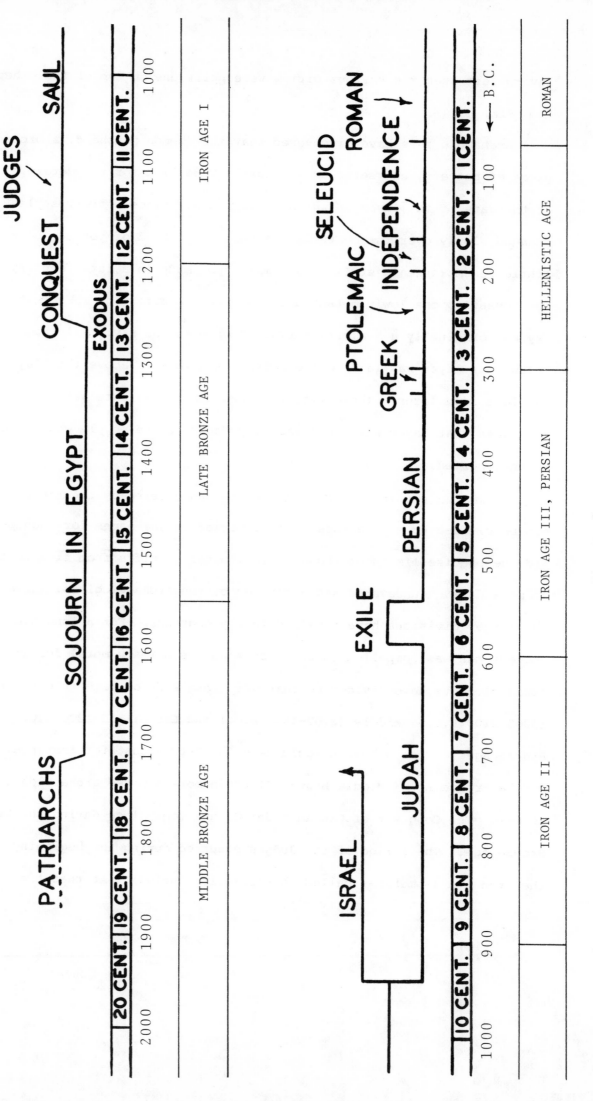

Fig. No. 5

the Philistines, who had settled on the coastland of Palestine, had brought

their knowledge of iron-making with them. They refused to allow the

Israelites this knowledge, and thus, for a time, the Israelites were

compelled to go to them for iron tools (see I Sam. 13:19 ff.). The

Iron Age is sometimes divided into three periods: Iron I (1200-900 B.C.),

Iron II (900-600 B.C.), and Iron III, or Persian, (600-300 B.C.). This

span of time includes the entire period of the Israelite state until

it was destroyed by the Babylonians at the beginning of the 6th century

B.C. The Hellenistic Period (300-63 B.C.) and the Roman Period (63 B.C.-

A.D. 323) have been given political names rather than names derived

from the materials man used for his implements.

Since the dating of the various layers of a tell cannot usually

be determined with enough precision to assign a specific year to them,

these archaeological periods are used instead. In practice all of the

large archaeological periods are further sub-divided into small

divisions. In many cases, when the sequence of pottery development

is thoroughly known, the date of a given potsherd can be narrowed down

to about fifty years. Thus a relatively accurate idea can be obtained

about the time-span in which one is working on a given layer. By

this means the archaeologists are able to obtain a great amount of

knowledge about the lives of the ordinary people in the biblical period.

b. COMPARATIVE STUDIES OF THE ANCIENT NEAR EAST

If the Bible is studied without regard for the cultural context

in which the events took place, a good deal of the insight into the

meaning of the Bible can be lost. The Bible was not written in a vacuum,

but in a particular place and at a particular time. The ancient Near

EVERYDAY LIFE

KINGSHIP

LAW

RELIGION

COMPARATIVE STUDIES OF NEAR EASTERN SOCIETIES

Kingship, religion, law and everyday life throughout the ancient Near East are studied and compared to the same aspects of Israelite life.

Fig. No.6

East was full of people other than "biblical" people, and that the lives of the people of Israel were influenced by those around them will come as no surprise. If this is true for the Old Testament, it is equally true for the New Testament, because the New Testament grew up in the context of the Judaism of the 1st century A.D. and in the context of the Hellenistic world which had been conquered by the Romans. The customs, beliefs and practices of all the surrounding peoples must be carefully studied in order to understand the cultural setting in which the Bible arose. This means that the religious and political structures, laws, and everyday life of the ancient Near East take on added importance for the biblical scholar. When these **facets** of the other cultures are compared and contrasted to the same aspects of life in the Bible, very interesting observations can be made (see Fig. No.6). For example, a study of kingship in Egypt and in Mesopotamia reveals marked contrast to the understanding of kingship in Israel. The laws found in the Code of Hammurabi throw light upon the legal background of the days of the Patriarchs. The study of the religious practices of the various cultures with which the people of the Bible came in contact reveal both similarities and sharp contrasts. Furthermore, a knowledge of the customs and practices of everyday life in the ancient Near East illuminate many biblical passages that would otherwise remain obscure.

2. LITERARY CRITICISM

In studying the Bible one deals not only with the historical aspect of the books but with their literary nature as well. The Bible is a collection of literature and a study of that literature will require the

use of a number of different but closely related disciplines. The
first of those disciplines with which we will deal is that of Comparative
Philology.

a. COMPARATIVE PHILOLOGY

Since the Bible was originally written in Hebrew, Aramaic, and
Greek, many problems arise when trying to translate these texts
accurately into modern languages. Sometimes the ideas which underlie
particular words are not evident on the surface of the English word
which is used to translate the biblical word, and as a consequence some
of the overtones of meaning are lost in the translation.

Take, for example, the word חָטָא (hata') in Hebrew (see Fig.
No.7). The primary meaning of that word is "to miss a goal" or "to
miss a way," as in "he who makes haste with his feet misses his way"
(Prov. 19:2). But this word is also used very frequently in a derivative
sense. One cannot only miss one's way, one can also miss the path
of right or the road of duty. In other words, one can "sin," and this
is precisely the meaning of this verb in II Chron. 6:22: "If a man
sins against his neighbor..." "Sin" is a missing of the mark or goal.
This Hebrew word has parallels which are directly related to it in
other Semitic languages such as Ethiopic, Syriac, Sabean, Arabic and
Assyrian. Although the scripts look strange to the untutored eye, the
consonants that lie behind those characters are either the same or are
closely related in all these languages. Therefore, Comparative Philology
tries to illuminate the Hebrew word by a comparison of the meaning of
the related words in the other languages of the linguistic family.

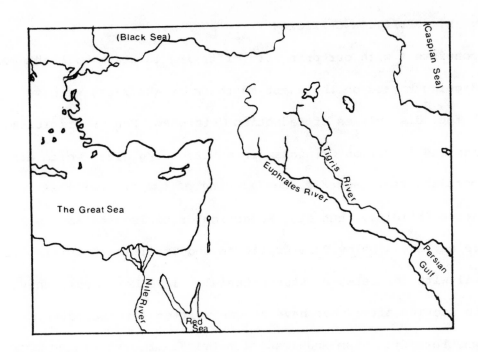

ETHIOPIC

ARABIC

Comparative philology is the study of words as they appear in the various languages which make up a linguistic family.

HEBREW

SYRIAC

ASSYRIAN

SABEAN

COMPARATIVE PHILOLOGY

Fig. No.7

b.   REDACTION CRITICISM

To be consistent with our principle of trying to start with the more concrete and going upward on the chart to the more abstract, we have arranged the four disciplines of Redaction Criticism, Source Criticism, Form Criticism and Tradition Criticism in an ascending order which aims toward the more abstract (see Fig. No.2). One of the reasons that not only Comparative Philology, but also Redaction Criticism and Source Criticism are on levels below Form Criticism and Tradition Criticism is that they deal with concrete, written material. In other words, they deal with the stories after they have become written literature. The other two, Form Criticism and Tradition Criticism, are placed above this level since, on the whole, they deal with the stories in the oral form in which they existed before they were written down--thus they are more abstract.

We deal with Redaction Criticism first because Redaction Criticism is interested in the literary work in its final and finished form (see Fig. No.8). The work of writing some biblical books could more aptly be classified as "editing" rather than "authorship." The writers frequently incorporated older materials into their works, not only so that these older works would be preserved, but also so that they could be used to further the ideas with which the editor was primarily concerned.

Redaction Criticism attempts to determine what the ideas of the editors actually were. It tries to study the editorial process itself. The editors included in their literary work a number of different elements. They incorporated such things as stories or documents that had already attained written form at the hands of some previous author. They included poems if those were appropriate. They added stories that had

100

Redaction Criticism attempts to elucidate the main ideas of the <u>editors</u> who compiled smaller literary units into larger ones. It is a study of the editorial process itself, with particular interest in questions such as, What was the editor's viewpoint? What were the questions he was trying to answer for his readers when he edited the material in this way?

REDACTION CRITICISM

Fig. No.8

hitherto only existed in oral form. But in the process of combining

the older materials, the editors also unintentionally left clues which

revealed their own motives for using the material in that particular way.

Redaction Criticism is primarily interested in such questions as: What

was the editor's viewpoint? Why did he use the material that was

available to him in this way? What were the questions he was trying to

answer for his readers when he edited the material in this fashion?

For example, in the Old Testament period the Deuteronomist set about

editing a very sizeable amount of material into a history, the point of

which would be to convey his own particular theological understanding of

the result of disobedience to the will of God. He lived in the 6th

century B.C., during the time when the Babylonians destroyed Jerusalem

and took the Jews off into Exile. He knew from first-hand experience

how important his message was because he believed this misfortune to be

the result of disobedience to God's commands. With great hindsight he

was able to see all of Israel's previous history in the light of those

disastrous times. Consequently, in editing this historical work, he

was able to use the material in such a way as to prove his point. He

used the already-existing book of Deuteronomy as the first volume of

his work, since it laid down the basic theological principles with which

he agreed. The later volumes of his history (Joshua, Judges, I and II

Samuel, I and II Kings) would be used to illustrate how those principles

had been at work from the time of the Conquest of Canaan up until his

own day.

What kinds of material did he incorporate into this large historical

survey? Where did those materials come from? Let us take one volume

of that history, the book of Judges, as an example (see Fig. No. 9).

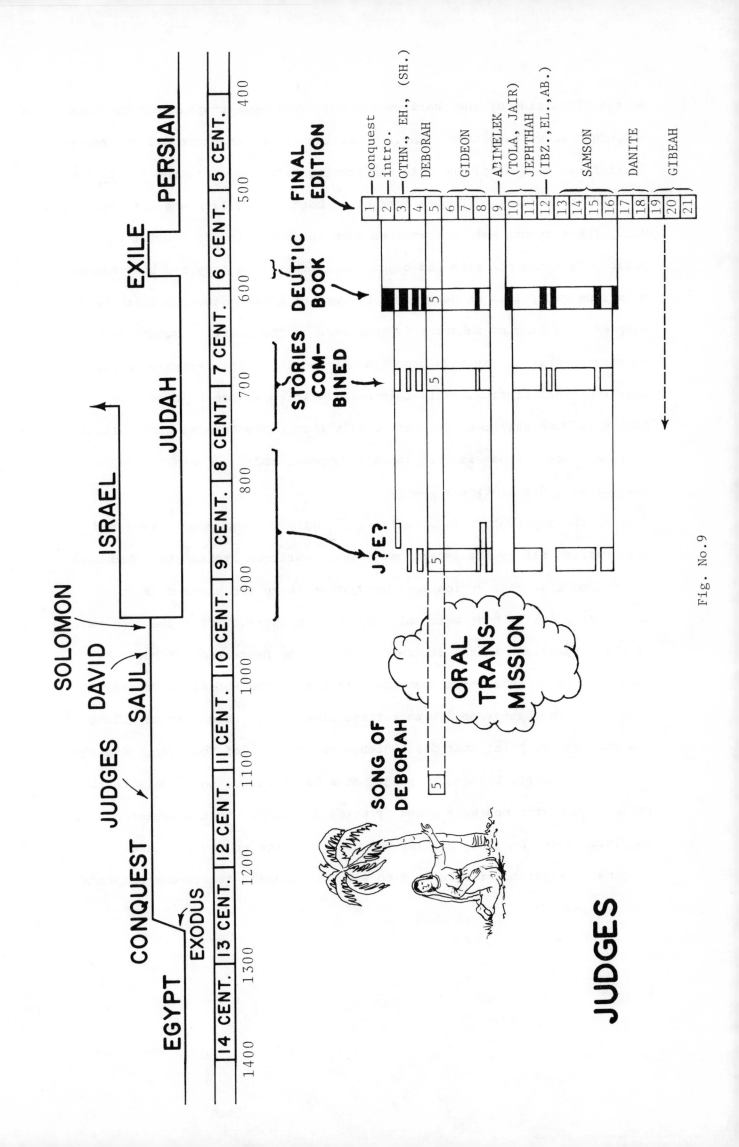

Fig. No. 9

JUDGES

On the right side of the chart we see the twenty-one chapters of the book of Judges as we have them today. Those twenty-one chapters did not reach their final form until the late 6th century B.C. However, the events described in the book of Judges took place back in the 12th and 11th centuries B.C. These events were not written down in manuscript form until the period after the monarchy had begun; until that time they had been handed down from generation to generation by word of mouth. (Notice that the 5th chapter, The Song of Deborah, is indicated on the chart in such a way as to suggest that it may have been transmitted in a more reliable fashion than the other stories. This chapter is written in poetic form, and poetry is much easier to transmit orally than prose because of its fixed, metrical form. Prose is more loosely composed and thus more liable to paraphrase and variation.)

In the 8th century B.C., after the northern kingdom of Israel had been carried off by the Assyrians, whatever written stories that had been saved from that destruction were brought south to the Kingdom of Judah and combined with those which already existed there. After the conquest of the Babylonians in the 6th century B.C., the Deuteronomist began his work. It is at this point that the interest of the Redaction Critic begins. The Deuteronomist took these stories and used them to illustrate his theological point that disobedience to the will of God brings disaster and that obedience brings blessing. At a later stage, sometime after the Exile, other sections were added by priestly editors to the Deuteronomist's completed work, but this editing was not extensive enough to change the original viewpoint. Thus we end up with our present twenty-one chapters of the book of Judges.

A similar process was carried out in the construction of the rest of the books comprising the Deuteronomic Historical Work. They all bear the imprint of the Deuteronomist's viewpoint and they show how he used these ancient oral traditions, written stories, poems, etc. for his own didactic and theological purposes. The Redaction Critic, then, is interested primarily in studying this process.

While our illustration has dealt only with works from the Old Testament, the principles apply equally well to the New Testament. The Redaction Critic is just as eager to ask similar questions of, say, the Gospel of Matthew or the book of Acts.

c. SOURCE CRITICISM

If the Redaction Critic is interested primarily in the motives apparent in the editorial work of the redactor himself, the Source Critic, on the other hand, is interested primarily in the written materials with which he worked. Often the biblical writers were faced with collections of ancient documents or traditions which paralleled each other in content but at times conflicted with each other in some of their details. Thus the writer had to make a decision as to what should be done. Should he put the mutually contradictory stories in sequence in his final work and let the reader puzzle over the inconsistencies? Should he choose one of the sources over the other and thus let the rejected source fall into disuse and perhaps disappear altogether? Or should he try to weave the two stories together so that no valuable evidence of the past would

Source Criticism studies the authorship and composition of biblical
literature with particular emphasis on isolating the written sources
that the writers used in their composition.

SOURCE CRITICISM

Fig. No.10

be lost? The writers of the Bible made all of these choices at one time or

another. It is the purpose of the Source Critic to study the literature of

the Bible with particular emphasis on trying to isolate these early written

sources which were used to make the final composition. In Fig. No.10 the

editor is combining two sources--one symbolized by x's and the other sym-

bolized by o's. The Source Critic attempts to unravel the resulting com-

bination into its original components.

The most famous and classic example of Source Criticism may be found

in the analysis of the sources that went to make up the first five books

of the Bible, the Pentateuch or Torah (see Fig. No.11). Around the 10th

century B.C. some writer in the south, perhaps in Jerusalem itself, began

to try to put in written form all of the oral traditions that were known to

him about the origins of the world and of the people of Israel. He probably

had only oral traditions upon which to draw, but these oral traditions had

been passed down faithfully for many generations. This anonymous writer

is called "J" by modern scholars because he consistently used the name

Yahweh (also spelled "Jahweh") for the name of God throughout his collection.

In Fig. No.11 his work is symbolized by a white scroll.

Some time later, possibly in the 9th century B.C. after Solomon's

United Kingdom had split up into the Kingdom of Israel in the north and

the Kingdom of Judah in the south, some northern collector also began

to write down all of the oral traditions which were known to him,

as his southern counterpart had done. His work is designated by the

letter "E" since he uses "Elohim" for the name of God in the earlier

part of his work. In Fig. No. 11 his work is symbolized by a light gray

scroll. In the 8th century B.C. the northern kingdom of Israel was

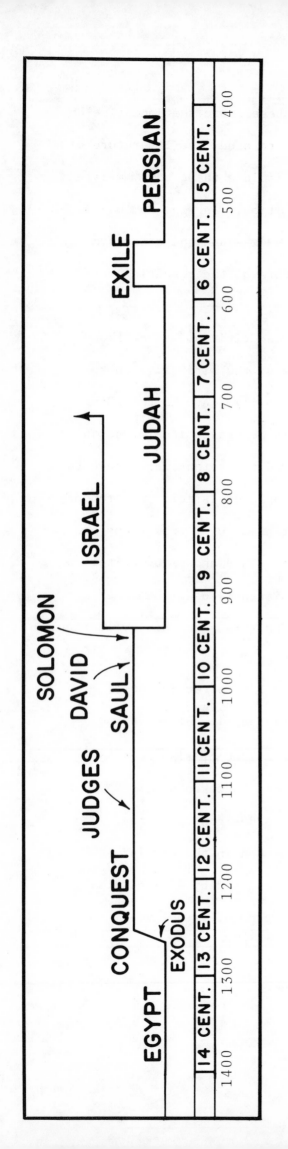

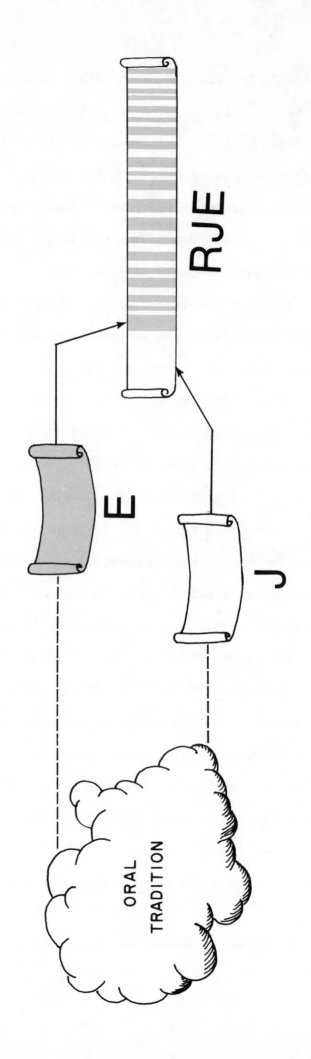

EGYPT CONQUEST JUDGES DAVID SOLOMON

EXODUS SAUL ISRAEL

JUDAH EXILE PERSIAN

14 CENT.	13 CENT.	12 CENT.	11 CENT.	10 CENT.	9 CENT.	8 CENT.	7 CENT.	6 CENT.	5 CENT.
1400	1300	1200	1100	1000	900	800	700	600	500	400

ORAL TRADITION

E

J

RJE

Fig. No. 11

destroyed by the Assyrians and the collection of E must have been brought down to the south in Judah to be preserved. Many of the E traditions were parallel to those of the J traditions of the south, though in some cases there were contradictions. Some editor in the south, probably in Jerusalem, decided that the collection was too valuable to be lost, and so, at the appropriate places, he inserted the northern material into the southern framework. He is designated as "RJE" because he is the redactor of the JE collection. In Fig. No.11 his work is symbolized by a scroll showing the combined sections of white (J) and light gray (E).

Later in the 7th century B.C. the book of Deuteronomy achieved its final form (see Fig. No.12), and this final form was in the shape of a sermon delivered by Moses in the period just preceding the Conquest of Canaan. This book reflected the ideas and attitudes of the 7th century B.C. but it put these ideas back into the time of Moses. Fig. No. 12 shows Deuteronomy as a dark gray scroll. Shortly afterwards, in the early part of the 6th century B.C. the Babylonians destroyed Jerusalem and its Temple and carried the Jews off into Exile. The priests who found themselves in Exile without a temple in which to offer sacrifices busied themselves by making collections of their ancient laws and ritual instructions. This work is symbolized by a black scroll in Fig. No.12. Some time after the Jews were allowed to return home in the 6th century B.C., some priestly editor decided to incorporate these collections of ancient priestly material into the collection which had been done by RJE. This editor is designated by RJEP because he is the redactor of the JEP collection. In Fig. No.12 his work is symbolized by the addition of the black sections to the JE scroll.

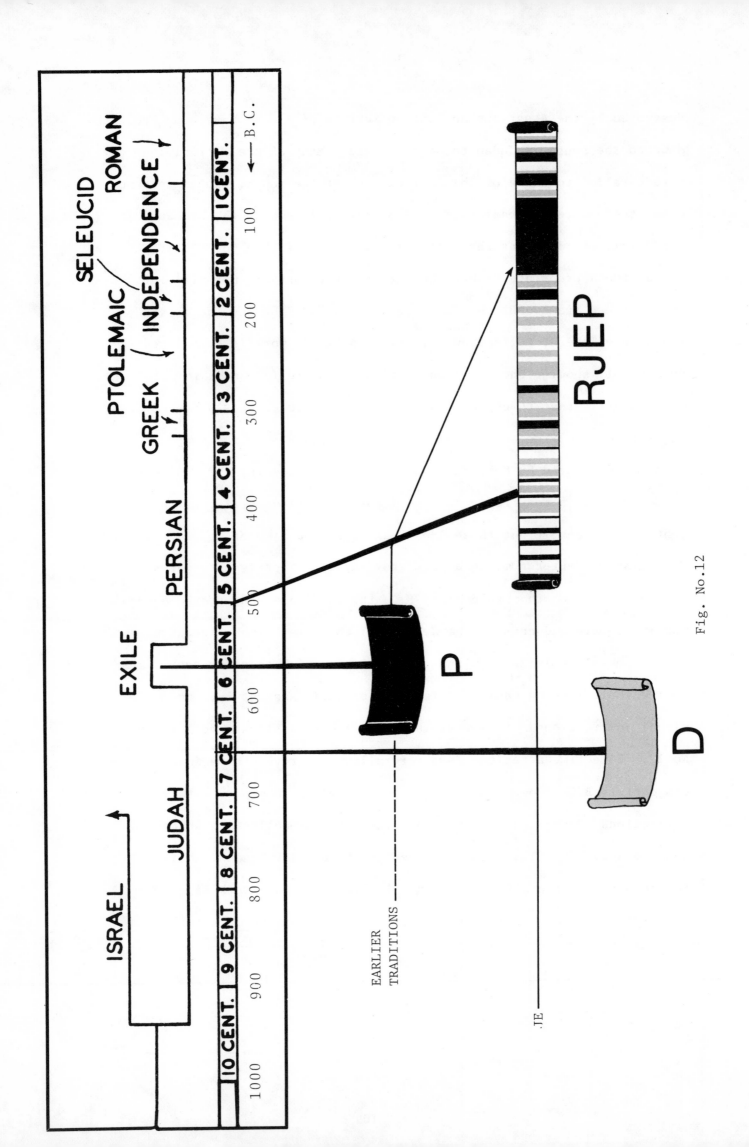

Fig. No.12

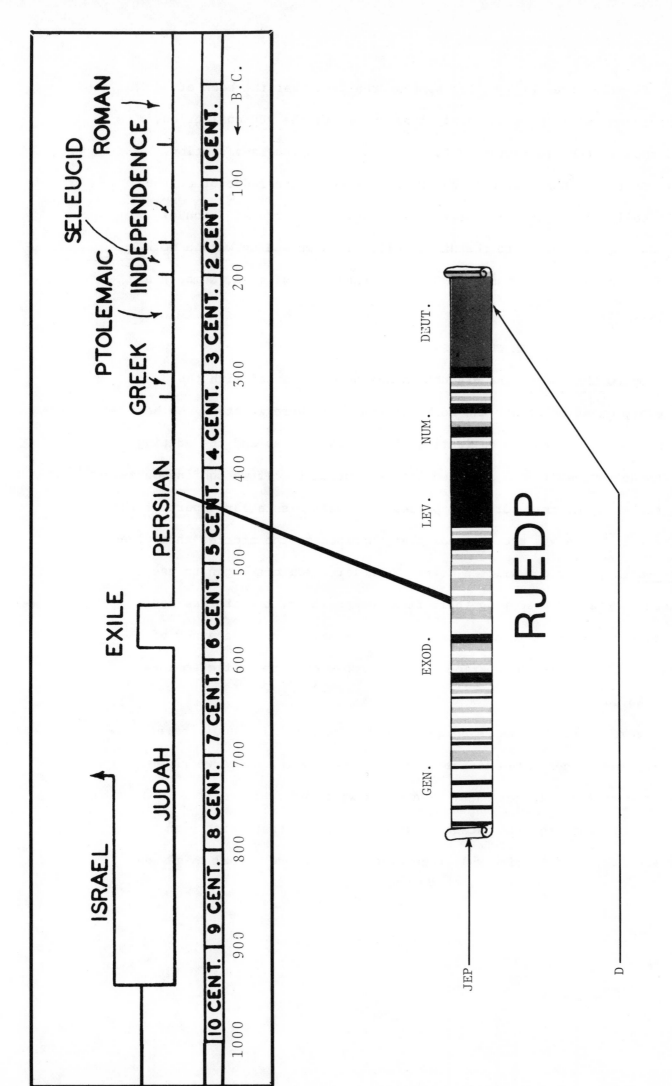

Fig. No.13

Finally, (see Fig. No.13) someone realized that the book of

Deuteronomy would make an ideal final volume to the JEP collection,

and thus in the 5th century B.C. it was added as the last section.

This editor is designated as RJEDP because he is the redactor of the

JEDP collection. The final torah is symbolized by the addition of

the dark gray section to the JEP scroll. Thus we end up with a work

which today bears the names of Genesis, Exodus, Leviticus, Numbers and

Deuteronomy.

d. FORM CRITICISM

Up to this point the discussion has been concerned with the

literary question of how the books of the Bible were written. We have

been concerned with the collecting of various sources and the editing

of those sources into a finished literary product. If we confine ourselves

to the study of this editorial process, we will miss a large part of the

picture. There was a great deal that happened to the stories themselves

before they ever got written down. When later editors began to use

these stories in preparing their final composition, the stories had

already undergone a long period of oral transmission. The study of

what took place in that period is the purpose of Form Criticism (see

Fig. No.14).

Form Criticism leaves on one side the larger, finished literary

units, and concentrates its attention on the smaller units which go

to make up these larger ones. Since the written version of the smaller

unit represents the last stage of development for that unit, Form

Critics try to determine what took place between the actual event and

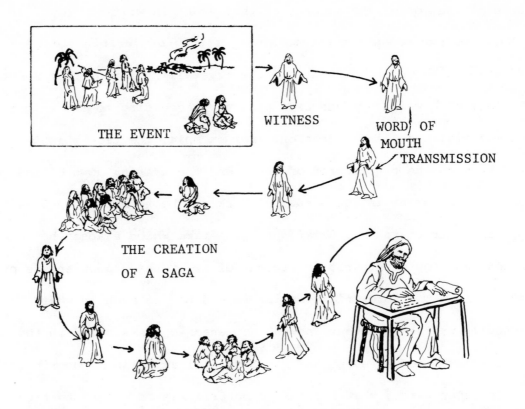

THE EVENT WITNESS WORD OF MOUTH TRANSMISSION

THE CREATION OF A SAGA

Form Criticism is a study of the smaller literary units (such as miracle stories, proverbs, healing narratives, sagas, laments, prophetic threats, hymns) which were used by the authors in their writing, as well as a study of how these units were handed down over the years in the community.

FORM CRITICISM

Fig. No.14

the crystallization of the account of that event in written form. In

Fig. No.14 we can see where the interest of the Form Critic lies.

The "distance" between the event and the crystallization of that event

in the form of a written manuscript will vary according to the nature

of the material under investigation. For example, the time which

elapsed between the crucifixion of Jesus and the writing down of the

account of that event in the Gospel of Mark may be no more than 35-40

years. In contrast to this brief span, the time which elapsed between

the Exodus and the first written account of it in the J document is probably

350-400 years. The Form Critic is interested not so much in what

was actually written down but in what happened to the stories in the

time between the actual event and its crystallization in manuscript

form. In other words, what happens to material as it is passed from

one person to another, either over a short period of time or over very

long periods of time? What factors shaped that material?

The Bible is full of small literary units, such as parables,

prophetic sayings, hymns, laments, healing narratives, proverbs, miracle

stories, etc. Form Criticism asserts that the meaning of a particular

literary unit is found not only in the "form" of that unit (parable, hymn,

etc.), but in the way in which that unit must have been used in a particular

real-life setting (the technical term is Sitz im Leben). The Form Critic

assumes that the use to which the story was put in real life would have

affected the interpretation and meaning of the material being transmitted.

In the New Testament, for example, the parables which were told by

Jesus were retold for a long time before they ever became part of a

written gospel. During that time they were used most frequently in the preaching of the early Church. The early Church did not exist in a vacuum, but faced real problems and issues. When parables were used in sermons in this oral stage, they must have been used in a fashion that would make them appropriate to that real-life situation. Thus when we look at a parable as it is written in a gospel, we must ask if we are hearing a verbatim account of the parable as Jesus first spoke it, or if we are hearing it as the early Church understood it in the years which immediately followed its first telling. Once we have determined what might be attributable to the early Church, we are in a better position to try to determine what the parable was in its original form. Obviously, this kind of study must take into account not only the liturgical background of the community which used these oral units, but also the anthropology and the social psychology of that community. Thus Form Criticism is intimately connected with a thorough historical study of the period as well as with the oral material under scrutiny.

e. TRADITION CRITICISM

Tradition Criticism is concerned with the study of specific biblical traditions and their development, whether in the oral or the written stage. It is concerned to ask questions such as:

1. What group was concerned with transmitting and shaping this material? Were they Priests, Prophets, or Wisdom Teachers, or were they some sub-division of one of these three groups? The answer to this

kind of inquiry will often reveal unexpected insights into the nature of the traditional material itself because of the differing theological presuppositions of each group.

2. <u>Where did this group operate geographically</u>? Once we are aware of the geographical locale of the tradition, we can frequently obtain a new understanding as a result of this information. For instance, was the group that was interested in transmitting this traditional material a group living in Israel or a group living in Judah? Both the northern and southern groups would have had their own peculiar assumptions and theological biases which would be important to uncover when studying the meaning of the tradition. Sometimes the locale can be even more specifically pinpointed. For example, the traditions concerning kingship and the Temple are intrinsically bound up with the city of Jerusalem. Other traditions, such as those of the Exodus from Egypt and the Covenant at Mt. Sinai, seem to be bound up specific-ally with the shrine located at Shechem. There were other specific traditions which were important to recall and preserve at shrines in such places as Gilgal, Dan, Beersheba, Bethel, etc. Once the tradition has been linked to a particular locale, new light can be thrown upon the nature of that tradition.

3. <u>Tradition Criticism,</u> like Form Critism, <u>is interested in the real-life setting</u> (<u>Sitz im Leben</u>)<u>of the tradition</u>. Both Tradition Critic and Form Critic must concern themselves with the religious, political and social factors which actually shaped that tradition in the real-life situation.

It is obvious from a thorough reading of the Bible that there

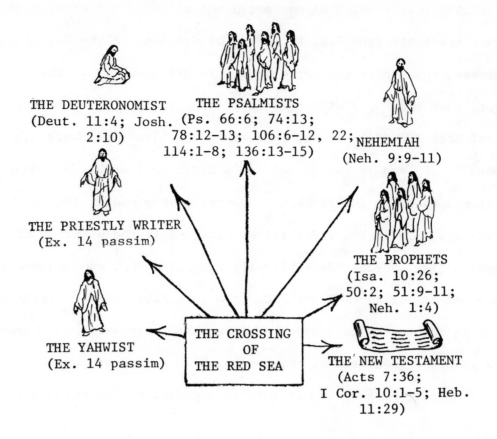

THE DEUTERONOMIST
(Deut. 11:4; Josh.
2:10)

THE PSALMISTS
(Ps. 66:6; 74:13;
78:12-13; 106:6-12, 22;
114:1-8; 136:13-15)

NEHEMIAH
(Neh. 9:9-11)

THE PRIESTLY WRITER
(Ex. 14 passim)

THE PROPHETS
(Isa. 10:26;
50:2; 51:9-11;
Neh. 1:4)

THE CROSSING
OF
THE RED SEA

THE YAHWIST
(Ex. 14 passim)

THE NEW TESTAMENT
(Acts 7:36;
I Cor. 10:1-5; Heb.
11:29)

Tradition Criticism is a study of how particular biblical traditions were used and interpreted by the various biblical writers in various periods of history. It is also concerned with the nature of the groups who transmitted the tradition, the geographical location of that group, and the real-life setting in which it lived.

TRADITION CRITICISM

Fig. No.15

are particular themes which appear again and again in different contexts throughout the Bible (see Fig. No.15). The Crossing of the Sea of Reeds, for instance, appears in all three great historical works of the Old Testament, each time in a different context. It appears in the Priestly Historical Work (Ex. 14), in the Deuteronomical Historical Work (Deut. 11:4; Josh. 2:10) and in the Chronicler's Historical Work (Neh. 9:9-11). But it also appears in the liturgical poetry of the Psalms (Ps. 66:6; 74:13; 78:12-13; 106:6-12, 22; 114:1-8; 136:13-15), the writings of the prophets (Isa. 10:26; 50:2; 51:9-11; Nah. 1:4), and even in the New Testament itself (Acts 7:36; I Cor. 10:1-5; Heb. 11:29). Tradition Criticism is interested in studying themes which reappear in different contexts in order to determine the use to which they were put in various periods of history and in various segments of the religious culture.

Tradition Criticism is particularly suited to the Old Testament because of the vast amounts of time involved in the transmission of the traditions. Its application to the traditions of the New Testament is somewhat restricted because of the relatively short amount of time covered by the New Testament period.

*   *   *   *   *   *

Thus the student of the Bible today has a number of tools at his disposal with which to study the Bible. These tools enable the student to get a glimpse into the intricacies of this amazing collection of books in a way that would not be possible without their employment. Each of these disciplines has produced a vast amount of literature on the various aspects of the Bible with which that discipline is concerned. The reader of such literature will find some conclusions with which he will not agree, and this is to be expected in any scholarly work. However, there will be much that will prove to be exceedingly enlightening, and such enlightenment could only have been obtained by employing these tools of Biblical Criticism.

EPILOGUE

We have done three things in preparation for the exploration of the Bible. We have looked at the books themselves to see what they contained (Section I); we have looked at the history which provided the context in which those books were written (Section II); and we have become acquainted with the various tools needed in such exploration (Section III).

If this volume accomplishes the purpose for which it was prepared, there will be fewer wrong assumptions made about the biblical material, fewer wrong turns taken in the process of studying that material, and, we hope, no instance of anyone's getting completely and thoroughly lost. However, one word of caution is in order. Many prospective travelers find the fascination of travel folders, tour-guide booklets, and maps to be so great that they settle for the safer and more comfortable mode of touring known as arm-chair traveling. No one will deny that this can be enjoyable and rewarding. But the ironical fact is that one misses the country itself and settles for descriptions of that country. The Bible is too exciting and rewarding to be experienced in any fashion but a first-hand encounter. If necessary, start your biblical traveling before having mastered the material in this book. Consult it when you begin to sense the need for it. But, by all means, travel. That is where the challenge is--not in the travel folders.